Trade in Health Services in South Asia

Arindam Banik
Editor

Trade in Health Services in South Asia

An Examination of the Need for Regional Cooperation

Springer

Editor
Arindam Banik
International Management
Institute (IMI)-Kolkata
Kolkata, West Bengal, India

ISBN 978-981-15-2190-4 ISBN 978-981-15-2191-1 (eBook)
https://doi.org/10.1007/978-981-15-2191-1

This Springer imprint is published by the registered company Springer Nature Singapore Pte Ltd.
The registered company address is: 152 Beach Road, #21-01/04 Gateway East, Singapore 189721, Singapore

To Amitayus

Preface and Acknowledgements

Trade in health services *aka* 'medical tourism' has attracted a great deal of policy interest in recent years with particular reference to South Asia. The apparent growth in this region has been fueled by a number of factors. Ease of travel and technological advances in information systems and communication allow patients to look for the treatment of a better quality at lower cost and more immediately from India. This has created further demand for the portability of health insurance cover, both public and private, due to patient mobility. However, there is a lack of hard research evidence on the role and impact of trade in health services in the context of South Asian economies despite its growing interests.

The study discusses the interaction of the demand for and supply of health services in South Asia. It highlights various organisations and groups involved in the industry. Treatment processes (including consideration of quality, safety and risk) and system-level implications for countries of origin and destination (financial issues and the impact on providers and professionals of cross-border trade in the health sector) are highlighted.

I would like to express my appreciation to Sarojakshya Chatterjee, Tirthankar Nag and Paramita Mukherjee for useful discussions on several occasions. Colonel Rafiqul Islam Mullick (Retired) deserves special appreciation for his continuous encouragement. I express my thanks to Solanki Sengupta, Librarian, International Management Institute, Kolkata, for her support. Mehr Khan provided invaluable assistance in the preparation of this manuscript. I am also immensely grateful to Sagarika Ghosh of Springer for her faith in me and her continued support despite delays in the execution of this project.

Finally, I would like to thank my wife, Mousumi, and my son, Amitayus, for providing a fresh sense of perspective during the study period.

New Delhi, India
September 2019

Arindam Banik

Contents

Editor and Contributors

About the Editor

Dr. Arindam Banik is currently Director of the International Management Institute (IMI), Kolkata, India deputed from International Management Institute, New Delhi. He is Distinguished Professor International Management Institute, New Delhi. He obtained his PhD from Delhi School of Economics in 1994, and went on to pursue his postdoctoral research at Manchester Business School and the Department of Economics, University of Cambridge (1994-95). He also taught at the Department of Economics, University of West Indies, Cave Hill Campus, Barbados (2000-2005). Professor Banik is a recipient of numerous awards, including the prestigious SANEI Research Award (by the World Bank and Global Development Network), and the University of the West Indies Campus Research Award for two consecutive years (2002 and 2003). He has worked as a consultant for various government and multilateral agencies including the World Bank, FICCI-New Delhi, International Development Research Centre (IDRC), ACC Mumbai, UNIDO, ILO, Indo-Canadian Cooperation Unit, GTZ and Government of India (Ministry of Rural Development), Caribbean Development Bank, and Government of Barbados. He has published more than 100 papers on international economics, macroeconomics, corporate governance and economic development. He has authored several books, including "Towards A Common Future: Understanding Growth, Sustainability in the Asia-Pacific Region" published by Palgrave-Macmillan, London, and articles for various magazines and newspapers. He is the editor of the respected management journal *Global Business Review*.

Contributors

Bhuban B. Bajracharya is Planning and Program Coordination Specialist at the Asian Development Bank, based in Kathmandu, Nepal. He has previously been associated with organisations such as UNESCAP, International Center for Integrated Mountain Development (ICIMOD) and ESAT/DANIDA.

Pradip K. Bhaumik, Professor of operations management, International Management Institute, New Delhi, is Fellow of the Indian Institute of Management, Ahmedabad, where his thesis was awarded the IFCI award for the best thesis proposal. He worked as Assistant Director and then as Deputy Director at National Productivity Council, New Delhi, during 1972–1978. He has been an active consultant to many companies—in both the private and the public sectors—as well as to international agencies like the US Agency for International Development, UNDP and GTZ. His research interests include areas like international trade, investment, innovation and R&D management, as well as topics like supply chain management, operations management, operations research and project management. He has pursued significant research in the area of FDI in the Caribbean, India and China, and authored (with Dr. Arindam Banik) the book *Private Capital Transfers to the Caribbean, India and China: Trends, Assessments and Determinants* (Palgrave-Macmillan, London, 2006). He has published many papers in reputed journals such as *Journal of International Development*, *Management Decision*, *International Journal of Social Economics*, *Savings and Development* and *Journal of Indian Business Research*.

Sahana Roy Chowdhury is Associate Professor of economics, International Management Institute, Kolkata. She has done her Master's and Ph.D. in quantitative economics from Indian Statistical Institute. She is Editor-in-Chief of the SAGE-based journal *Studies in Microeconomics*. Her research interest lies in development economics, labour economics, public policy and fiscal policy issues. She has more than 8 years of post-doctoral experience in research and teaching, and has published in several international and national journals of repute. She has worked at NIPFP (Macro-Finance Division), Delhi; ICRIER, Delhi; and ICRA Ltd. (Monetary Research Project Division) and was a visiting scientist at Cornell University, USA. She has delivered invited lectures at the University Paris-Est Marne-la-Vallée, Paris, on Indian macro-developmental and fiscal issues and labour market issues. She has worked with the Expenditure Management Commission formed by the Ministry of Finance–Department of Economic Affairs in 2014 and provided key research inputs to the commission. She has served as an expert panellist in the research meeting on employability organised by the Centre for Policy Research in Higher Education, New Delhi (Department of Educational Finance—under MHRD, GOI).

Gaurav Kumar Jha is Indian Economic Service officer. He is currently posted as Deputy Director, Indian Economic Service Cadre, Department of Economic Affairs, Ministry of Finance, Government of India. His research interest lies in subjects related to agriculture and food management, labour economics, economics of health and education and public policy.

He has pursued his Master's in Economics from Delhi School of Economics and is a graduate from Shri Ram College of Commerce. He has served the Indian Government in different capacities. He has worked as Assistant Director in the Expenditure Management Commission and has rendered policy inputs for the Commission. Has also served as Assistant Director, Economic Division, Department of Economic Affairs, wherein he was involved in providing inputs and advice for policy formulation pertaining to agriculture, social infrastructure and employment sector. Prior to joining the Indian Government, he has worked as Business Analyst at Hewlett-Packard. He also holds the experience of Assistant Professor at Shri Ram College of Commerce and the Hindu College University of Delhi.

Sheikh Md. Monzurul Huq is Professor in the Department of Geography and Environment, Jahangirnagar University, Savar, Dhaka, Bangladesh. Has authored many books and is a known researcher in Bangladesh. His research interests include tourism geography and medical geography.

Paramita Mukherjee is Professor (economics) and Dean (academics) at International Management Institute, Kolkata. As an alumnus of Presidency College, Kolkata, she has completed MS in quantitative economics from Indian Statistical Institute and Ph.D. from Jadavpur University. She has 21 years of experience in industry, research and academics, with stints at AC Nielsen (formerly ORG MARG), ICRA and renowned business schools. She teaches courses on economics, finance and econometrics. Has conducted MDPs with CII, Kolkata, and has handled consulting assignments as well as research projects. Her research interest lies in financial economics and applied econometrics. She has worked on contemporary issues in financial sector and authored a number of research papers in international journals of repute.

List of Figures

List of Tables

Chapter 1
Introduction

Arindam Banik

South Asian countries are having a large intra-regional trade in health services. However, a large part of health services trade in the region is informal, whereas the formal health services trade, which is rather small in size, faces a large number of barriers—implicit or otherwise. The measurement of barriers to trade in services, and the gains associated with removing such barriers, has been of keen interest in recent years, particularly ins the context of inclusion of services and investment in South Asian Free Trade Agreement (SAFTA). In general, barriers to trade in health services are unlike tariffs. They are typically regulatory barriers, rather than explicit taxes. The underlying economic rationale for these policy reforms is that the removal of barriers to trade in services is likely to result in lower prices, improved quality and higher competitiveness. As with trade in goods, restrictions on trade in services reduce welfare because they create a wedge between domestic and foreign prices, leading to a loss to consumer surplus. Health services liberalization exerts an economy-wide influence as they constitute strong inputs to all other economic activities, including trade. Some studies identified several challenges related to the implementation of General Agreement on Trade in Services (GATS) commitments.[1]

[1]Interestingly, multilateral liberalization of trade in goods has taken place for the last half century. However, liberalization of trade in services began only in 1994 with end of Uruguay Round. The General Agreements on Trade in Services (GATS) is the first and the only set of multilateral rules covering international trade in services. The agreement was concluded at the Uruguay Round (1986–1993). It came into force in January 1995. The GATS sought to gradually liberalize and expand trade in the service sector. It had a "built-in agenda" mandating members to kick off progressive liberalization negotiation on services from January 2000. The Guidelines and Procedures of Negotiations were adopted by the Council for Trade in Services on March 2001 as provided in the GATS Article XIX: 3; see Kelegama (2009).

The authors would like to express their deepest gratitude to the South Asia Network for Economic Institutions (SANEI) in Kathmandu, Nepal for allowing us to use some contents of the Chaps. 1, 3, 6 and 7 of the report entitled, "Trade in Health Services in South Asia: An Examination of the Need for Regional Cooperation", submitted by the authors. Our heartfelt thanks to Dr Vishnu Dev Pant, Co-ordinator SANEI for support.

A. Banik (✉)
International Management Institute, Kolkata, India

A. Banik (ed.), *Trade in Health Services in South Asia*,
https://doi.org/10.1007/978-981-15-2191-1_1

It seems useful to mention here that through the GATS, the member states of the World Trade Organization (WTO) have the option to commit themselves to liberalize health services. Article I of the GATS, following Bhagwati (1984) and Sampson and Snape (1985), discusses a four-part typology of trade in health services (Bhagwati 1984; Sampson and Snape 1985, quoted in Findlay and Warren 2000). In terms of the GATS, health services include medical and dental services, services provided by midwives, nurses, physiotherapists and para-medical personnel, hospital services and other human services.

The four modes of GATS delivery of health services are: (1) *cross-border supply,* where the service is provided remotely from one country to another, such as telemedicine via Internet or satellite, or international health insurance policies[2]; (2) *consumption abroad,* where individuals use a service in another country, such as patients travelling to take advantage of foreign healthcare facilities[3]; (3) *commercial presence,* where a foreign company sets up operations within another country in order to deliver the service, such as hospitals, health clinics or insurance offices[4] and (4) *presence of natural persons,*[5] where individuals such as doctors, nurses or midwives travel to another country to supply a service there on a temporary basis.

[2]The rising competition for foreign patient has been accompanied by initiatives in the marketing of medical institutions. Such initiatives, sponsored by governments, universities or private firms, consist of dissemination of information on the institutions and patients. For example, the so-called health tourism fairs are one of the most common mechanisms used by governments and institutions, either directly or through marketing agencies. Likewise, a telemedicine link has been established between Apollo Hospitals at Hyderabad, Delhi and Chennai in India and Lahore Medical Imaging Center, Lahore in Pakistan. This is the first telemedicine link between India and Pakistan. Such kind of link is an excellent effort, which will go a long way in bringing together the medical community and people of the two countries. This will enable people of Pakistan to have easy access to specialists and superspecialists without travelling to India. The telemedicine link has been launched in a move to facilitate exchange of medicare and health facilities at reduced cost in South Asian countries. The Apollo Telemedicine Networking Foundation has also established telemedicine centres in Nepal and Sri Lanka.

[3]A good number of patients come to India from Bangladesh, Nepal, Bhutan, Sri Lanka, Pakistan and Afghanistan for medical treatment every year. Likewise, many patients come to Pakistan from Afghanistan for the medical treatment. Lack in domestic health infrastructure forces the Bangladeshi patients to move to India for treatment. In general, Mode 2 (consumption abroad) is the most popular mode through which trade in health services has been taking place between the two countries.

[4]For instance, in an effort to enhance domestic capabilities in medical services as well as reduce foreign exchange costs derived from outflows of patients, several Asia Pacific countries are allowing foreign medical institutions to establish "local branch campuses" or "subsidiaries". For example, India's Apollo Group has opened branches in Bangladesh and Sri Lanka, and Escorts Heart Centre in Bangladesh, Nepal and Sri Lanka.

[5]International trade in health services focuses on the mobility of patients; no comprehensive information on the movement of medical professionals is adequately available. A similar lack of information exists in relation to cross-border supply of medical education services. As mentioned, ample demand for health services, triggered by the needs of the labour market, and the emergence of new technologies are rapidly expanding the market share of telemedicine. Such an expansion is likely to have a growing international component, but its potential for changing the current patterns of trade in the sector is difficult to assess at this stage.

There is a dearth of analytical research in estimating barriers to trade in health services, particularly in the context of South Asia. This study observes that an in-depth study exclusively focusing on health services trade will not only strengthen overall services trade capacity of South Asian region but will also promote global as well as regional trade.

Objectives

South Asian economies have small intra-regional trade in health services, but mostly in informal sector. The trade in health services is directly associated with language, culture, technology and also with some extent ethnicity and religion. These types of asymmetries across the countries pose a great threat to trade in health services. In view of technological change, there is an important need to measure the market size and also the barriers to health services trade in South Asia.

Therefore, the main purpose of the study is aimed at understanding the structure of heath services and their assessments and economic costs of barriers to trade in health services in selected South Asian economies such as Bangladesh, India, Pakistan, Sri Lanka and Nepal.

The literature on trade in services remains vast in general but found to be small in health services, specifically in the context of South Asia. However, a few of them have some contributions in this respect. For example, De and Bhattacharya (2007) and Banik and Bhaumik (2014) focus on health-related infrastructure issues and then discuss dominance of informal trade in this context.

Interestingly, India, Thailand, Singapore and Malaysia are the most preferred countries. According to various statistics, Indian High Commission in Dhaka had issued 130,000 medical visas until October 2017, which is double the figure registered over the same period last year. In fiscal year 2015–2016, India saw 460,000 inbound patients at its different hospitals, according to Export of Health Services survey conducted by Directorate General of Commercial Intelligence and Statistics of India. Of them, 165,000 were from Bangladesh as against 58,000 medical visas were issued to Bangladeshi nationals. It is useful to mention here that Bangladeshi patients contributed 35% of the total foreign patients in India in 2017. As regards revenue, this had contributed about 50% of the total revenue earned by Government of India due to medical services, thus making it the largest contributor to medical and health tourism of India.[6]

In another interesting study, Kelegama and Mukherjee (2007) find that the Indian doctors face problems in obtaining work permit in Sri Lanka for their stay in that country.

[6]A recent estimate of Bangladesh Investment Development Authority reveals that Bangladeshis spend $2.04 billion annually on health care abroad. The amount is estimated to be 1.94% of the country's GDP; see https://www.dhakatribune.com/feature/health-wellness/2017/11/30/doctor-trust-bangladesh.

Banik and Bhaumik (2014) have recently studied Service Trade Restrictive Index (STRI)[7] in the context of five South Asian economies such as India, Pakistan, Nepal, Sri Lanka and Bangladesh. The authors focused their analysis based on sectors such as education, health, travel and tourism, telecom (fixed and mobile) and transport sectors (air and maritime). They found that trade restriction in health sector varies across South Asian countries. For example, aggregate scores for select South Asian countries range from 0.23 (Nepal, the least restrictive) to 0.41 (Pakistan, the most restrictive). Pakistan's score is primarily attributed to consumption abroad (Mode 2) and movement of natural person restrictions (Mode 4). On close investigation, it appears that Central Bank's lengthy formalities to allow foreign exchange for nationals' treatment in other countries beyond limit are the major impediment. Bangladesh follows with an aggregate STRI score of 0.35, comprised of restrictions across Modes 2 and 4, but almost full openness in Mode 2. India's aggregate score of 0.33 reflects the sector's relative openness, carrying restriction in Mode 4.

Outline of the Study

Baring Afghanistan and Bhutan, South Asian countries are World Trade Organization (WTO) members and are committed to multilateral liberalization in services trade. They have committed to the rules and principles of the GATS, where Article V of GATS permits the liberalizing of trade in services between or among the parties to an economic integration agreement. However, within trade in services sector, the liberalization of health services has seen little progress, particularly among developing countries.

Services have emerged as the engine of growth in the major South Asian economies explaining the dynamism displayed by them over the past decade. Service sector is also emerging as an important source of employment. In general, the trade potential of services remains to be exploited by the region. In many sectors, a

[7]The STRI methodology which translates qualitative information on services barriers into an aggregated quantitative score by sector is based on four modes defined by the GATS. This categorization also allows one to capture the issue of complementarity and substitution between modes. The authors have gathered qualitative information through questionnaires completed by government agencies and various country reports that are available in the region as well as supplementary research. The qualitative information has been used to determine the values of the different components of the sectoral aggregate and modal indexes. The weight of each component has been determined through pair-wise comparison. The transition from qualitative to quantitative analysis involves many benefits, but is not without risks. The two main benefits of synthesizing qualitative information in a quantitative index are first, to enable the comparison of restrictions across countries at the sectoral level, and second, to determine the impact of barriers on trade in services and on different variables of economic performance. This provides a more objective basis for domestic policy debates, as well as for bilateral, regional and international negotiations through more transparent evaluations of reciprocity in concession-making. The main risk, however, of such an exercise is that a traditional researcher faces when moving from qualitative information on policy to a synthetic quantitative index: some dose of subjectiveness. The methodological improvements proposed by researchers on these subjects such as the use of pair-wise comparison techniques try to minimize the subjectivity.

strong domestic market plays a key role as the platform for developing export capacity. This pattern is evident in telecommunications, audiovisuals, distribution, health, transport and related services and higher education services—and even, in some cases, in e-commerce-related sectors. Normally, countries tend to follow a pattern: serving the domestic market first and building on that export markets. South Asian countries need to take steps to specialize in services sectors which have potential for expansion in domestic markets and build their export capacity. Regional cooperation and integration of the service markets in the South Asian Association for Regional Cooperation (SAARC) region may also assist in specialization and strengthening the competitiveness of services industries in the South Asian countries (SAARC Secretariat 2008).

Given that the health services are traded predominantly through patient mobility across borders (consumption abroad), nonetheless, a host of problems persist in South Asian countries in opening up their health services, in raising their health services providing standards, in recognizing each others' standards and in removing the barriers to trade in health services. It is important to bear in mind that cross-country disparities in health services may not only reflect different policy priorities, but also a variety of economic, social and demographic factors.

Health services sector liberalization exerts an economy-wide influence as they constitute strong inputs to all other economic activities, including trade. Health services are the least committed sector in WTO. In India, Modes 2 and 4 in health services are unbound under market access and national treatment for hospital services, whereas in the case of Nepal and Pakistan, only Mode 4 is unbound. Ideally, effective health service liberalization requires quality services and cost reduction among and within countries. Health patients need to consider both barriers (inner and outer) while framing any international policy. There is also an in-built need to look into the subject in a wider context of regional trade initiatives when South Asian countries have decided to include services trade and investment in SAFTA.

South Asian countries have great potential in health services trade. They have undertaken a substantial degree of liberalization in trade in health services autonomously over the past decade and a number of commitments under GATS to bind their reforms multilaterally. However, a number of regulations and barriers still exist that may need to be addressed in the context of SAARC for fully exploiting the synergies that may exist for mutually beneficial exploitation. Besides regulations, taxation policies with regard to services also need to be examined. However, the information based on different aspects of domestic policies and regulations that affect market access to health services in a country is scanty and needs to be addressed in the framework of cooperation.

Trade in Health Services—An Overview

Better health services enable countries to face the challenges of environment and global commercial integration. Evidence confirms that expanding economic opportunities for people living in developing and LDCs raises their incomes. The key to expanding their economic opportunities is to help them build up their assets. Human capabilities such as health are of intrinsic value and also have powerful effects on material well-being. Broad access to such facilities is also important to the material prospects of the people. And the trade in health services can reduce their vulnerabilities. Therefore, challenges for the South Asian countries are to achieve gender equality health—national commitment, and to recognize each others standards—international commitment.

In case of national commitment, the prospects for achieving gender equality in health vary considerably between countries. There has been more progress in gender equality in health (World Bank 2005). Still, more than a third of developing countries will not achieve gender parity in health, and most of them risk not meeting the Millennium Development Goal (MDG) if they do not take immediate action to extend health services to cover poor people. The risk is greatest for sub-Saharan Africa and South Asia, the regions reporting the slowest progress in universal health.

In case of global commitment, progress towards mutual recognition of health services differs across countries. While developed countries were successful in recognizing each others' medical services, the problem gets more acute in case of developing and less developing economies may raise their incomes. Specifically, a strong asymmetry persists in terms of standards and contents of the medical services across the countries and regions. In addition, changes in the domestic and international market structures have promoted the appearance of activities closely related to health services. These new activities are designed to support health processes or systems without being "instructional activities" per se. Examples of these activities are exchange programmes in health services and health services education services. In some countries, these activities are considered to constitute health services. Given the pace of change in the sector, definitional issues have also appeared as an important issue in many countries.

Health services also exist as a "private consumption" item with a price determined freely by the providing institutions. Private sector expenditure on medical institutions reveals significant variations among OECD countries, ranging from 2% or below of total expenditure on health in Portugal, Sweden and Turkey, to over 22% in Germany, Japan, Korea and the USA (WTO 2001). Private sector expenditure is particularly significant at the tertiary level of health amounting, for instance, to over half of total private expenditure on health in Japan, Korea and the USA.

Health services have become the single largest sector in many economies worldwide. It not only provides the bulk of employment and income in many countries, but also serves as vital input for producing other goods and services. So an efficient health services sector is crucial for the overall economy. And because of this, agreement on opening up health services markets is crucial to the success of the current global trade talks.

Such market opening will bring gains to all economies, including the developing world, as long as it is done in a carefully considered way. But opening up health services markets is a particularly complex challenge. For one thing, any discussion of trade in health services has to include the thorny question of in- and out-migration issues (e.g. whether a qualified medical professional can freely move from one country to another to provide services to the patients).

In South Asia, Afghanistan, Bangladesh, Nepal, Pakistan and Sri Lanka are showing to import interests in health services. A cooperative framework may facilitate SAARC countries to tap advanced expertise available in some countries such as India through use of technologies such as tele-medicines etc to hospitals in other SAARC countries (SAARC Secretariat 2008). Trade in health services can be enhanced through Mode 2 (patients seeking treatments in other countries), Mode 3 (investment in laboratories and hospitals) and Mode 4 (temporary movement of health professionals like doctors and specialists). As mentioned earlier, cross-border informal trade in health sector plays a very important role in the case of services.

Another problem is that there is analytical literature which purports to show that when intermediation services are explicitly represented in their true economic form, rather than being represented in ad valorem equivalent form, the two fundamental theorems of welfare economies need not hold. Because of this property, welfare impacts from liberalization in services trade (even in small open economies) can be negative rather than positive as generally presumed in the goods like models used in the literature. Ryan (1990) study may be considered as an early piece to point this out. Chia and Whalley (1997) provided an example of welfare worsening liberalization in the case of trade liberalization in banking services. Bhatterai and Whalley (1998) have shown how explicitly modelling telecom liberalization in a network structure can change perceptions as to the division of the gains from liberalization between small and large countries. The implication seems to be that only limited confidence can be attached to results obtained from the ad valorem equivalent modelling used in numerical literature because the analytical structures used rule out alterative results. This problem would arise even where the results of individual studies are not contradictory with one another. Nevertheless, due to lack of information on cross-country trade in health services, we have not come across any concrete study with clear focus to measure barriers to trade in health services in case of South Asian countries.

Our study is based on both secondary and primary sources. As regards primary sources, we have collected information from Indian doctors and hospitals involved in trade in health services. We also conducted a detailed survey of foreign (South Asian) patients who came to India to receive health services due to India's growing importance in supplying health services in the region. We surveyed a sample of 190 such patients based on convenience sampling procedure. Detailed information regarding their diseases, treatments, costs and payments was collected based on a questionnaire designed to capture all relevant data on patients including their perception on some aspects of trade in health services. Similarly, we surveyed 20 hospitals and 12 doctors. On demand side, we have added country-specific studies such as Bangladesh, Pakistan, Sri Lanka and Nepal, highlighting the key issues in trade in health services in order to identify some policy suggestions.

The remainder of the book is laid out as follows. Chapter 2 demystifies catastrophic expenses in Indian healthcare sector. Chapter 3 discusses healthcare sector in Bangladesh. Chapter 4 examines health sector scenarios in Sri Lanka and their policies and implications. Chapter 5 investigates health sector scenarios in Pakistan and their policy priorities and challenges ahead. Chapter 6 analyses overall structure of healthcare sector in Nepal. Chapter 7 highlights India's emergence as a major destination of quality healthcare centre. Chapter 8 contains conclusions and policy recommendations.

Chapter 2
Demystifying Catastrophic Expenses in Indian Healthcare Sector

Paramita Mukherjee

Introduction

India has initiated the process of moving towards Universal Health Coverage (UHC) in recent years. The objective of UHC is, on the one hand, to ensure that everyone, poor and rich alike, should have access to essential healthcare services (called service coverage) and on the other hand, one who receives needed healthcare, should not face undue financial hardship (called financial protection). In a developing country like India, achieving both is not an easy task. For example, catastrophic expenses, which are the measure of financial protection, are defined as the share of out-of-pocket (OOP) expenses in a family's income or consumption expenditure exceeding 10%. Low incidence of such catastrophic expenses either may indicate that people have access to needed health care and they are protected from OOP expenses, or may imply that people are not having access to needed health care and are not paying for it! So, in order to make such a scheme successful, both the aspects have to be considered.

The role of OOP expenses in the context of India is very important as the higher incidence of such expenses is potentially devastating for majority of the population and may push them to impoverishment. So, in order to address the two aspects and build a sound healthcare system for all, an efficient financing strategy is essential. There may be two types of strategies, viz. supply-side and demand-side strategies (Hooda 2017). Under the supply-side financing strategy, health services are provided through public healthcare system, financed mostly by taxation by the government, whereas the demand-side strategy focuses on financial protection through insurance, so that people have access to health care irrespective of the provider, public or private. In India, there has been a distinct shift from supply-side to demand-side strategies in recent times, i.e. towards financial protection that is likely to reduce the impoverishing effect of OOP expenses.

P. Mukherjee (✉)
International Management Institute, Kolkata, India

A. Banik (ed.), *Trade in Health Services in South Asia*,
https://doi.org/10.1007/978-981-15-2191-1_2

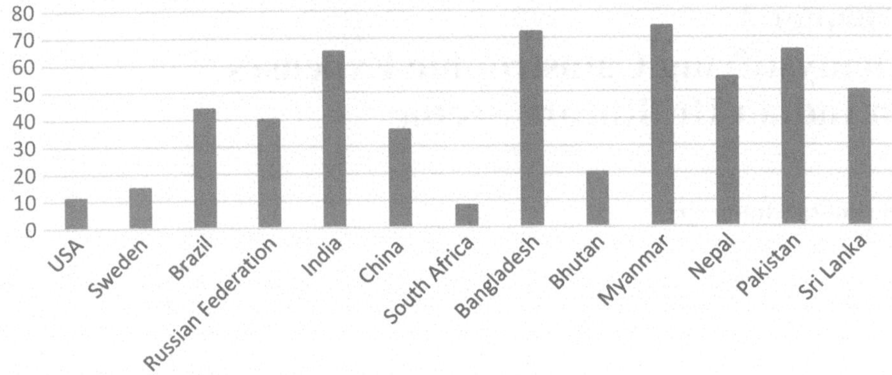

Fig. 2.1 OOP as % of CHE, 2016. *Source* WHO

In India, OOP expenditure as a proportion of current health expenditure (CHE) has reduced from 72% in 2000 to 65% in 2016 (WHO Global Health Expenditure Database). However, compared to global standard, it remains substantially higher in India. It is the highest among the BRICS, with South Africa at 8% and the rest ranging between 36 and 44%. Among the South Asian countries also, Bhutan, Nepal and Sri Lanka have much lower percentage of OOP (Fig. 2.1), compared to India.

It is pertinent to look at the possible causes of such a high ratio of OOP expenditure to CHE in India, despite a number of initiatives and projects launched by the government over the decades. This is important because for success of UHC, this may provide valuable insights about both the demand-side and supply-side strategies. Also, there is ample evidence that high incidence of OOP expenditure on health is capable of becoming catastrophic and leads to impoverishment of a large section of the population. For example, Hooda (2017), based on the Consumer Expenditure Survey (CES) data, points out that the share of OOP spending in total household spending has risen from 3.93% in 1993–1994 to 6.77% in 2011–2012. Moreover, owing to such health payments, 4.66% of the population fell below the poverty line across India. Dieleman et al. (2017) estimate that the per capita health spending in India is going to increase to USD 629 in 2030, from USD 253 in 2014 and further to USD 1138 in 2040. However, it is estimated that along with an increase in government spending as a share of total spending on health from 31.3% in 2014 to 43.7% in 2040, OOP spending as per cent of total spending is expected to come down from 65.6 to 54.3% during the same period.

There exists a negative correlation between the proportion of people experiencing catastrophic health payments and the amount of funding by the government in the form of pre-payment (Pandey et al. 2017). Before the announcement of *Ayushman Bharat* that encompasses UHC in 2018–2019 budget, a number of publicly funded schemes in India did exist; so one may be curious why such catastrophic health expenditure remains to be so high in India. Theoretically, the possible causes may be many: *first*, government spending may be declining. If that is the case, next question is whether the provision of health infrastructure is declining or the pre-payments in the form of insurance are not rising. It may also happen that infrastructure is not expanding, and subsidisation of the publicly provided health facilities has been curtailed. Alternatively and more plausibly, the rise of private sector in provisioning of health services and the continuous increase in the cost of such services may also contribute to rising OOP expenses, at least for higher-income groups. *Second*, if government spending on insurance payment is not declining, then the insurance coverage may not be sufficient or the targeted group may not be getting the benefits. *Third*, over the decades, incidence of some diseases might have gone up leading to higher OOP expenditure. *Fourth*, if the incidence of diseases has gone up, whether these diseases are covered under insurance adequately is an important question. *Finally*, the catastrophic health expenditure may also depend on a number of macroeconomic and health system indicators, which are beyond the purview of this chapter. Given this backdrop, this chapter focuses on explaining the high OOP expenditure on health in India and its implications for the strategies to achieve UHC. The present chapter tries to demystify the high level of OOP health expenditure by looking at the four possibilities mentioned above. The chapter also looks at some of the international experiences of implementation of UHC and tries to find out the lessons from those experiences that may be applicable in the Indian context.

The chapter is structured as follows: the next section focuses on some evidence on catastrophic health expenditure in the recent past. Section "Government Spending on Health" focuses on the government spending on health, followed by the section on the experience of implementation of UHC in select countries. Section "Conclusion" concludes the chapter.

Evidence on Catastrophic Expenditure

OOP payments are the primary means of financing health care in most of the low-income countries, and India is no exception. One of the widely accepted measures of financial protection under the Sustainable Development Goals (SDGs) is catastrophic out-of-pocket expenses. Large OOP expenses, viz. 10 and 25% of total household expenditure, are catastrophic. A second indicator of financial protection is medical impoverishment which estimates the poverty implications of catastrophic expenses.

The household OOP expenses in India have increased substantially from USD 14,017 million in 2000 to USD 53,629 million in 2016 (WHO Global Health Expenditure Database). There are umpteen numbers of studies, which estimate both the incidence of catastrophic expenditure and medical impoverishment in the context of India. Ghosh (2010), based on the National Sample Survey Organisation (NSSO) data on consumption expenditure for 1993–1994 and 2004–2005 for Indian states, observes that on an average household spending as proportion of total consumption expenditure increased to 5.5% in 2004–2005, from 4.4% in 1993–1994. Across states, medicines accounted for 61–88% of total OOP spending. Interestingly, it was observed that the low-income states spent higher proportion on medicines, while the higher-income states spent higher proportion on inpatient care. Also, both the incidence and intensity of impoverishment have increased in 2004–2005, with 4% households falling into the catastrophic bracket (by the standard of 25%), compared to only 2.8% in 1993–1994. Hooda (2017) finds that the share of OOP spending in total household spending increased further to 6.77% in 2011–2012 and per capita OOP spending has increased among households for both rural and urban as well as both the poor and the rich. Moreover, the poverty deepening effect of OOP payments is higher among rural households than urban, with monthly per capita consumption level of below poverty line (BPL) households dropping by Rs. 27.8, in 2011–2012. The impoverishment is observed to be the highest in Uttar Pradesh.

In some other studies, too, similar evidence exists. For example, Pandey et al. (2017) observe that there has been an increase in the proportion of households experiencing catastrophic health spending during 20 years till 2014 with greater increase for poor compared to rich. Moreover, the proportion was highest among households with older people, and the incidence is higher in rural households. In a similar study, Selvaraj et al. (2018) find that total OOP payments and medicine OOP payments were catastrophic for 17.9 and 11.2% households in 2011–2012, indicating the affected households to be 29 million. Drugs OOP payments pushed 3.09% into poverty during 2011–2012. They also observe that when it comes to the OOP spending in India, the most common health condition for seeking outpatient care was fever, followed by cancer and injuries and for inpatient care, childbirth and cardiovascular events. Keane and Thakur (2018) also estimate that while poverty fell during 1999–2000 to 2011–2012 in general, medical impoverishment has increased, with 4.1% of population being in the state of "hidden poverty" owing to medical spending when OOP medical expenses are treated as necessary expenses, not a part of consumption.

Wangstaff et al. (2018) estimate the catastrophic health spending in 133 countries including India and observe that globally, the proportion of population incurring catastrophic medical payment increased from 9.7% in 2000 to 11.7% of world population in 2010. With such evidence of increasing incidence of catastrophic spending and impoverishment, it is important to look into it in depth. Interestingly, it is observed that in countries with similar kind of health system, incidence of catastrophic spending may not be the same, e.g. countries like UK, Canada, Armenia and Azerbaijan officially cover 100% of their population with public health services, but the incidence of catastrophic spending in the first two is less (2–3%) than the latter two (16% and 8%, respectively). Such a variation in incidence is also observed across countries like Hungary, South Korea and Romania, despite the national health insurance scheme officially covered 100% of the population. Contrary to this, in the USA, insurance coverage rates remained nearly unchanged, but the incidence of catastrophic spending fell during 1995–2013. There is another important finding that when a fraction of population with insurance coverage increases, it does not always lead to a fall in catastrophic payments, e.g. it did fall for Mexico, Thailand and Vietnam, but not in China, Indonesia or the Philippines. More importantly, it was found that the incidence of catastrophic spending is positively associated with per capita GDP and share of GDP spent on health at least for lower income levels, and negatively associated with the share of total health expenditure channelled through social security funds and other government agencies. Another curious result points to the fact that the role of private insurance and other non-profit institutions is questionable as there is no evidence that health payments made through such channels (funded through voluntary premiums/contributions) provide financial protection. In such a context, the role of public financial protection arrangements, funded by taxes and mandatory insurance contributions, assumes great significance.

Government Spending on Health

The increasing incidence of OOP health spending, coupled with the significant role of financial protection, implies a very important role of government spending on health. Also, the move towards UHC in India will involve significant role of government spending. According to WHO Global Health Expenditure Database, the share of current health expenditure (CHE) in gross domestic product (GDP) in India has gradually declined from 4.03 to 3.62% between 2000 and 2016, whereas the share of health capital expenditure in GDP has risen slightly from 0.1 to 0.5% during the same period (Fig. 2.2). The ratio of general government health expenditure to GDP remained to be less than 1%, though it has shown an increase from 0.83 to 0.93% during 2000–2016.

Looking at the components of CHE, in 2016, domestic general government health expenditure as a proportion of CHE is at 25.4%, compared to 20.7% in 2010, while the share of domestic private health expenditure in CHE has fallen from 76.6 to 73.5% (Fig. 2.3). During the same period, the share of external health expenditure in CHE has fallen from 2.7 to 1%. The private health expenditure, the major component, on the other hand, consists mostly of OOP health expenses (at 65.2% of CHE in

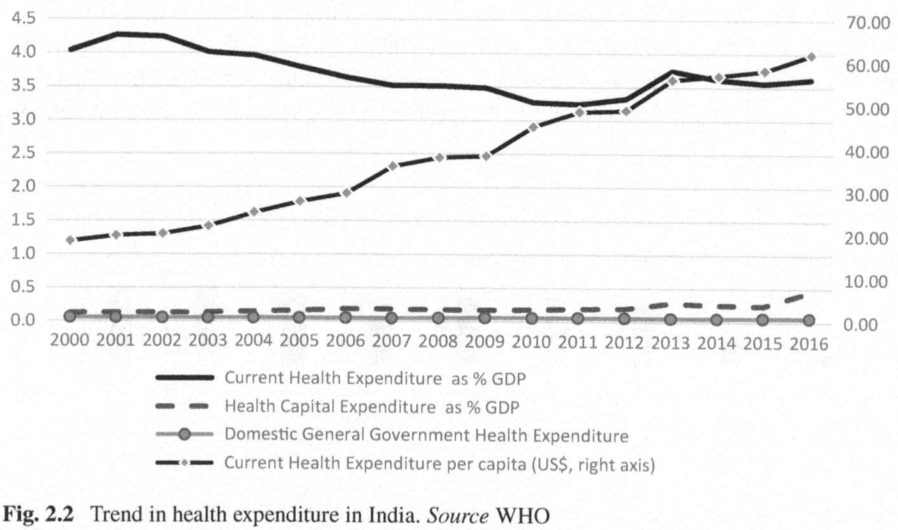

Fig. 2.2 Trend in health expenditure in India. *Source* WHO

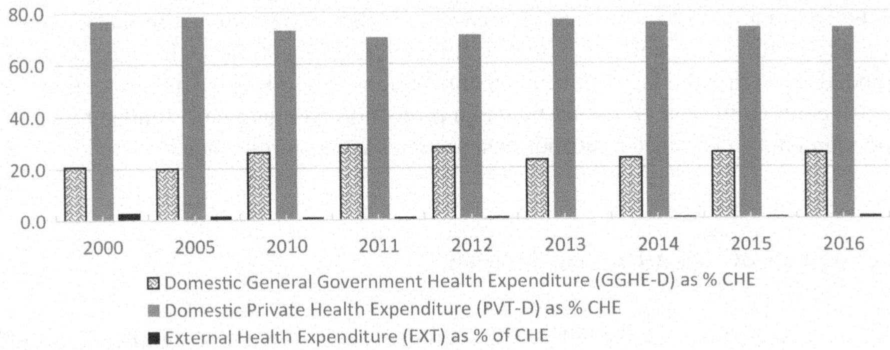

Fig. 2.3 Composition of current health expenditure (%). *Source* WHO

2016), voluntary health insurance (at 4.5%) and other private health insurance (at 4.6%). During 2000 and 2016, there has been a noticeable increase in voluntary health insurance (Fig. 2.4). It is also interesting to note that though the per capita government and private health expenditure have recorded substantial increase over the past decade, the share of government health expenditure in total government expenditure has remained more or less the same, from 3.3 to 3.1% during 2000–2016 (Table 2.1).

In this context, it is not unexpected that the share of government financing arrangements in CHE remained more or less the same over the period of 2000–2016 (at 21.6% in 2016), with the share of compulsory/social health insurance going up from 1.6 to 3.2%. However, voluntary financing arrangements remained to be the major source of financing, with a meagre drop from 77.4 to 74.9%. If we look at the CHE across healthcare functions, in 2016, around 34.4% is spent on inpatient curative care followed by 28.7% on medical goods and 17.7% on outpatient curative care (Fig. 2.5). Similarly, Fig. 2.6 shows that, of domestic general government expenditure across healthcare functions 61.2% is spent on curative care (inpatient and day care combined), followed by 25.2% in outpatient curative care and 10.1% on governance,

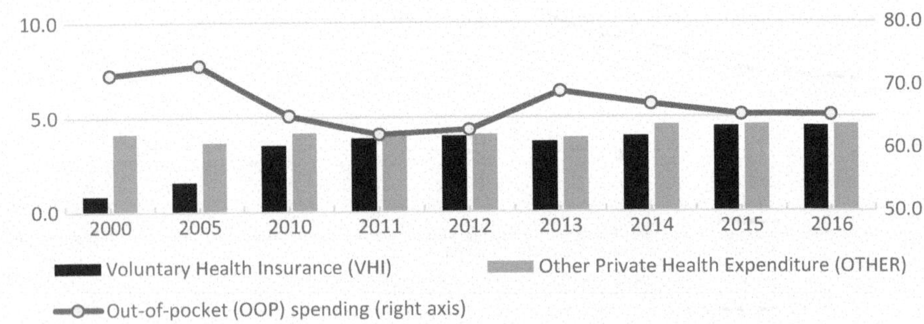

Fig. 2.4 Components of private health expenditure (all as % of CHE). *Source* WHO

Table 2.1 Trend in domestic general government expenditure

	2000	2005	2010	2011	2012	2013	2014	2015	2016
Domestic general government health expenditure (GGHE-D) as % general government expenditure (GGE)	3.3	3.0	3.2	3.5	3.5	3.1	3.0	3.1	3.1
Domestic general government health expenditure (GGHE-D) per capita in US$	3.8	5.6	11.9	14.1	13.7	13.0	13.5	15.1	15.9
Domestic private health expenditure (PVT-D) per capita in US$	14.2	21.7	33.0	34.2	34.9	43.1	43.2	43.4	46.1

Source WHO Global Health Expenditure Database

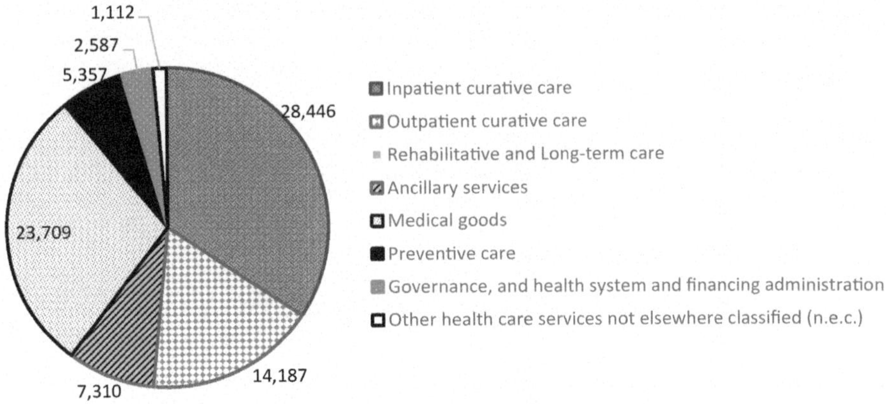

Fig. 2.5 CHE 2016 by healthcare functions, USD million. *Source* WHO

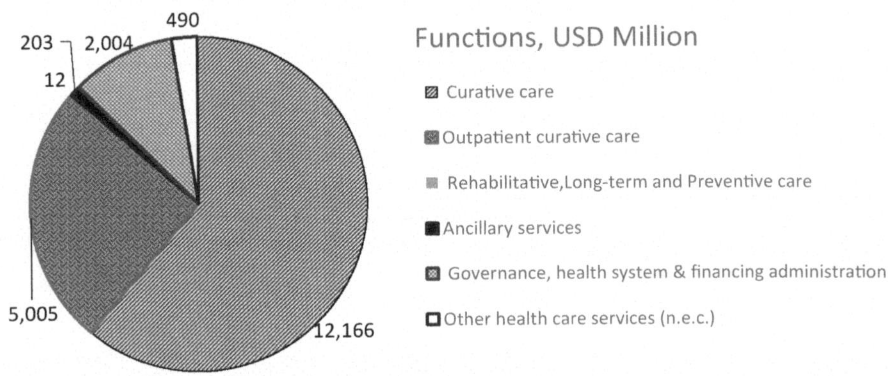

Fig. 2.6 Government expenditure 2016 by healthcare functions, USD million. *Source* WHO

health system and financing administration in 2016. These probably imply that the need for healthcare for events other than hospitalisation events are a substantial portion of the health expenses and majorly financed by voluntary health insurance and OOP expenses.

In India, health is a state subject as per Constitution, and it is pertinent to look at the health spending of state governments over the years. Revenue expenditure on medical and public health and family welfare as a proportion of total revenue expenditure for all state governments taken together has been on decline since 2002–2010 and then gradually rose and is at 5.3% in 2018, slightly less than that of 2002 (Fig. 2.7). More importantly, if the same revenue expenditure on health is viewed as a proportion of developmental revenue expenditure, it steadily declined from 9.4% in 2002 to 7.4% in 2011, followed by a gradual and slow rise reaching 8.3% in 2018. Table 2.2 presents the capital expenditure on health by all state governments, which

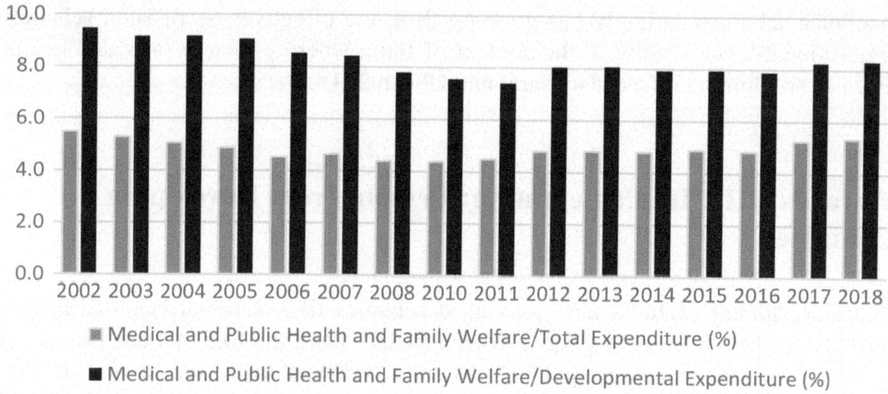

Fig. 2.7 Trend in state government revenue expenditure on health in India, all states. *Source* RBI Report on State Finances: A Study of Budgets, several issues

Table 2.2 Trend in government expenditure on health—all states

	Medical and public health and family welfare/Total revenue expenditure (%)	Medical and public health and family welfare/Developmental revenue expenditure (%)	Medical and public health and family welfare/Capital expenditure (%)
2002	5.5	9.4	3.0
2005	4.9	9.0	2.1
2010	4.4	7.5	2.9
2015	4.9	7.9	3.2
2018	5.3	8.3	3.8

Source RBI Report on State Finances: A Study of Budgets, several issues

as a proportion of total capital expenditure, follows the same trend of a drop till 2010 from 2002 and then rising again. It currently stands at 3.8% in 2018.

The government health expenditure including the capital expenditure stands at 1.18% of GDP in 2015–16, much lower than its counterparts of BRICS nations. Out of this total government health expenditure, the share of the Union Government is 35.6%, and State Government share is 64.4% (National Health Accounts Estimates, 2015–2016). Also, the ratio of government health expenditure to total health expenditure stands at 30.6% in 2015–2016, which itself speaks of inadequacy of financial protection and/or the provisioning of health infrastructure for all. In absence of public provision of such infrastructure, the private sector has served the people who could afford the services, and the OOP expenses are still high.

Given that the official data on health expenditure has just started coming in and is not comparable with a time series of previous years, it is difficult to infer or analyse the role of health spending on infrastructure and insurance/social security. However, Ghosh (2018) observes that at least for select schemes, public expenditure on health insurance schemes certainly has gone up. But, the effectiveness of such schemes is questionable, especially in the context of India where privately provided health services are dominant (see also Barai and Ghosh 2018).

Towards UHC Implementation: Lessons from Developing Countries

The Government of India has announced schemes like National Health Mission (NHM), Rashtriya Swasthya Bima Yojana (RSBY) and the like that are conceived to be the pillars of achieving UHC. Though NHM is fairly recent one, RSBY was launched in 2008 which targeted the coverage of BPL families. Ghosh (2018) observes that RSBY had a target of covering entire BPL population by 2012, but even in 2018, only 50% were covered. It is alleged that the insurer did not reach out to all the eligible population and a fraction was made aware of the state-sponsored schemes. Moreover, those who were covered did not utilise the scheme to the fullest extent for various reasons. Also, impact evaluation studies could not find any reduction in OOP expenses due to coverage of RSBY (Karan et al. 2017). This raises doubt about the effectiveness of publicly financed health insurance schemes as evidences show that most of the payments went to private hospitals; public healthcare delivery system received a small fraction of it. So, the targeted health insurance along with a healthcare delivery system dominated by private providers has failed to provide financial risk protection and access to healthcare needed. In such a scenario, the question is, for India, with increasing focus towards insurance coverage of the government, what should the way ahead be.

It is pertinent here to mention the experience of some developing countries. Universal basic health care, which some poor and developing countries have already implemented without extra financial burden, can be a solution in the Indian context. Moreover, it is not only affordable; the community health workers can play a significant role in making a difference in health care in low-income countries. Universal basic health care is about achieving health for all through taxes or by mandating the public to buy insurance and thus, requires the rich, young and healthy people to subsidise the poor, the old and the sick. Countries like Thailand and Rwanda have observed significant improvement in healthcare outcomes and/or fall in OOP expenses by adopting the universal basic health care. Chile and Costa Rica have similar life expectancy as USA, but spends only one-eighth of what USA spends on health per person. Rwanda introduced such scheme for over 90% of the residents, and the infant mortality has declined from 120 per 1000 live births in 2000 to under 30 in 2017.[1]

Thailand also has a life expectancy close to the rich countries in OECD after it implemented Universal Coverage Scheme which covers 98% of population. The scheme was accompanied by reforms like incentives for doctors for working in rural

[1] Within reach, *The Economist*, April 28, 2018, p. 11.

areas and extra payments to hospitals to take patients.[2] Yet, Thailand spends only 4% of GDP on health which it used to spend even 20 years back. Rwanda covers 90% of its population in terms of health insurance that gives access to community health services and treatments; most visits have a co-payment, and there is a tiered system of premiums with exemptions for the poorest. Thailand, in 1980s, froze capital investment in big hospitals and focused on primary care centres, which cut mortality rates. In Ethiopia, since 2004, training of "health extension workers", who are simple high school graduates, took place, and they have been able to cut child and maternal mortality significantly. Rwanda also has gone for community health workers at every village.[3] Therefore, with more or less the same government spending on health, it is feasible for a country to achieve better performance in terms of access to healthcare and reduction in OOP expenses through universal basic health care.

Conclusion

The chapter tries to find out the scenario of health care in India in the light of the possible implementation of UHC. Several studies as well as the data from different official sources indicate that in India, though the government spending is picking up in terms of insurance coverage in recent years, we have not been able to cover 100% of even BPL population and leave alone above poverty line (APL). The existing schemes have also not succeeded in achieving the desired objectives and targets. Private financial insurance fails to provide financial protection and the public financial protection arrangements where not only the higher proportion of people is covered, but also the full extent of payment is covered, become very important. *Second*, government allocation on health out of total government expenditure has not risen over the years, and private health expenditure as well as voluntary health insurance is the dominant source of health spending and financing. Though state governments have started increasing their allocation of resources on health gradually and social security contributions are slowly picking up, these are grossly inadequate. *Third*, given the publicly provided healthcare facilities are inadequate and privately provided facilities are not affordable by considerable proportion of the population, adopting universal basic health care may be a solution.

Finally, taking cue from the experiences of low-income and developing countries, India may think of providing primary health care for all and creating "community health workers" by providing basic medical training and small incentive to anganwadi workers to take care of basic health care for all in publicly provided primary healthcare centres where services are provided free of cost. Gradually, the coverage may be extended to more complex healthcare services. This might be a step forward to achieve desirable health outcomes as well as reduce the incidence of catastrophic expenditure and impoverishment over time. Moreover, this will not involve extra

[2]The price of human lives, *The Economist,* April 28, 2018, p. 12.

[3]Special Report, *The Economist,* April 28, 2018.

financial burden on the government, but may ensure basic health care for all. Since such community health workers operate at the local level, creation of awareness about general health, diseases as well as prevention of certain diseases will also be possible. Developing countries have proved that low income and comprehensive health care are not mutually exclusive. Hence, in India, instead of relying on publicly financed health insurance schemes and high-cost privately provided healthcare services, policy-makers should focus on more efficient use of government funds through targeting universal basic health care in achieving the objective of access to healthcare and financial protection for all.

Chapter 3
Health Sector in Bangladesh

Sheikh Md. Monzurul Huq

Introduction

Although expansion of trade and investment is a common goal of the South Asian Association for Regional Cooperation (SAARC) bloc unfortunately, it is lagging behind in regional cooperation in trade and investment in health services. Cooperation among the member countries of SAARC is stressed for strengthening and creating competitiveness and specialization among the South Asian countries (SAARC, Secretariat 2008). Out of eight countries of the SAARC region (countries are: Afghanistan, Bangladesh, Bhutan, India, Maldives, Nepal, Pakistan and Sri Lanka), six are members (excluding Bhutan and Afghanistan) of the World Trade Organization (WTO). Among the countries under SAARC region, Bangladesh is a net importer of health services.

With an overview of the health service sector of Bangladesh, this case study focuses on health service trade in Bangladesh and possible regional cooperation to enhance health service trading in the SAARC region. It also examines the rules of the GATS and focuses on the pattern of trade in health services in Bangladesh. This case makes an effort to examine the barriers and opportunities in health service trade for Bangladesh under the four modes.

This chapter has similarity of the previous publication with SANEI (The South Asian Network of Economic Research Institute). Permission has been obtained from the rights holder in order to reuse copyright chapter.

S. Md. Monzurul Huq (✉)
Department of Geography and Environment, Jahangirnagar University, Savar, Bangladesh

A. Banik (ed.), *Trade in Health Services in South Asia*,
https://doi.org/10.1007/978-981-15-2191-1_3

Methodology

This study used a multi-method design (Waitzkin et al. 2005) which involved data collection from three sources: (a) research and literature on trade, public health and health services such as professional journals, newspapers, government documents, corporate records, international organizations and from the Internet; (2) interviews conducted with people involved in the private hospitals (e.g., hospital administrators) and telemedicine service providers, officials from trade ministry, persons from the professional organizations (e.g., medical association); and (3) interview (checklist) conducted with health service consumers who received services from local hospitals (private and government) and foreign hospitals (patients received services from Indian hospitals).

Key informant interviews were conducted in person with semi-structured protocol, designed to elicit responses concerning causes and problems of employing foreign doctors in Bangladesh by the health service providers and prospects and barriers to trade in health service in Bangladesh under four modes of GATS. Total of four administrators from four private hospitals (hospitals A, B, C and D), which employ foreign doctors and nurses, were interviewed as key informants to gather information about the present situation of the foreign doctors and nurses working in these hospitals and their opinions about the causes of employing foreign doctors and nurses and problems associated with their employment.

It is understood that an analysis of the perception of the patients would provide significant information regarding causes behind the pattern of health service trade at the regional and country levels. To examine the barriers in trade in health services in Bangladesh and South Asia as a whole, patients' perceptions about health services in Bangladesh hospital and foreign countries were examined and compared. Total of 81 patients were selected who received health services from various hospitals (30 patients, who received services from private hospitals; 28 patients who received services from government hospitals; and 23 patients who took services from Indian hospitals).

Patients were interviewed with a multi-response checklist containing total of 17 questions. Sample size of the study was derived through snowball sampling method. In this study, snowball sampling technique is considered as most appropriate method, as it was impossible to locate the respondents without getting information from any source. For this reason, an initial small group of respondents was selected first with random method, and after being interviewed, these respondents were asked to identify others who belong to the target population of interest. Subsequent respondents were selected on the basis of referrals (Malhotra 2008). This study used Mean Score of Relative Importance (MSRI) technique, a simple statistical method to analyze data. The data were coded as BD_Govt_MSRI for government hospitals, BD_Private_MSRI for private hospitals in Bangladesh and INDIA_MSRI for Indian hospitals.

The respondents were asked to rank each possible answer with a score from 1 to 17. These answers were then tabulated and analyzed with Mean Score of Relative Importance (MSRI) statistical method to assess the variations in the importance of the factors that were mentioned by the respondents who received services from private and government hospitals in Bangladesh and also from Indian hospitals. It is understood that the variations in the relative importance score would help to assess the underlying causes of consuming health services in India by the Bangladeshi patients.

The case study further attempts to examine the nature of barriers to trade in health services, based on available qualitative evidence and administering checklist interview. It also tries to see current perception on optimal regulatory policy in health service sector and examines the links between domestic regulation and trade in Bangladesh.

Overview of Health Service in Bangladesh

Bangladesh is administratively divided into 6 divisions, 64 districts, 507 Upazilas (sub-districts), 4484 unions and 87,319 villages. In the public sector, the largest health service provider of the country is the Ministry of Health and Family Welfare (MOHFW). The MOHFW has established a countrywide network of physical and organizational infrastructure to plan, manage and deliver public health and family planning services. The macro-level health policy and planning are prepared by this ministry. There are also two major implementation wings under the MOHFW—the Directorate General of Health Services (DGHS) and the Directorate General of Family Planning (DGFP). The types of public health service facilities provided by these organizations are mentioned in Table 3.4. The service providers in this respect include teaching hospitals, district hospitals, Upazila health complexes, union health and family welfare center and community clinics serving a huge number of population of the country (Table 3.12).

The DGHS registered 1005 private clinics and hospitals in 2005 (DGHS 2009, http://www.dghs.gov.bd/). The number of medical colleges, dental colleges and institutes of health technologies in private sector was 34, 10 and 39, respectively, in 2008 (DGHS 2009, http://www.dghs.gov.bd/). A large number of people avail private health services in the country, as public health services are backward and not reliable in many respects. Table 3.5 depicts the list of key public and private healthcare providers of the country. Besides public and private health service providers, there are quite a few non-government organization (NGO) hospitals and clinics operating in the country (Table 3.13). Table 3.14 depicts the pattern of health workforces available in the country.

The total per capita expenditure on health as percent of GDP is quite low in the country, and private health sector spending is high in comparison with the public sector (Table 3.15). It should be noted that the private hospitals represent a small portion of the hospital capacity of the country (Tables 3.1, 3.2 and 3.3).

Bangladesh's health system is dominated by public sector, in terms of health services infrastructure consisting essentially of hospitals. Various economic factors, such as the distribution of income, wealth, distribution and consumption processes,

Table 3.1 Types of health service facilities in Bangladesh

Level of care	Administrative unit	Health facility	Population coverage
Tertiary referral level	Division (6) or district	Teaching hospitals/institutes (19): 250–050 beds each	10–15 million population
Second referral level	District (64)	District hospitals (59): 50–150 beds each	1–2 million
First referral level	Upazila (507) Urban Upazilas do not have UHC	Upazila health complexes—UHCs (399): 31 beds each	200,000–450,000
First-level health facility	Union (4484) UH & FWCs are not established in 397 unions where UHCs exist	Union Health and Family Welfare Centre—UH & FWC (3200)	21,000
First contact with health services/health providers	Ward (13,209)	Community clinics—CC (18,500) each with one family welfare assistant (FWA) and one health assistant (HA)	6000
	Village (87,319)	Trained birth attendants (TBAs) and village health volunteers	1000–1500

Source Bangladesh Health Bulletin (2001), Directorate General of Health Services of Government of Bangladesh

Table 3.2 Key healthcare providers in Bangladesh

Government of Bangladesh	Private	NGOs
University and medical college hospitals	Private clinics and hospitals	NGO hospitals
District hospitals	Private practitioners	NGO clinics
Upazila (small administrative unit) health complex	Traditional providers	
Union health and family welfare center	Homeopathic providers	
Community clinics	Unqualified providers	
Specialized hospitals	Drug retail outlets	
Other facilities	Retail sale of other medical goods	
Health facilities in other ministries and autonomous corporations		

Source World Bank (2005)

Table 3.3 Workforces in the health service sector in Bangladesh

Number of workforces	Total
Total number of registered doctors	47,259
Estimated total number of doctors now available in the country	38,537
(a) Percentage of doctors working under the MOHFW (b) Percentage of doctors working under other ministries (home, police, railway, civil aviation, LGED, social welfare and labor)	35% 3%
Percentage of doctors working under the private sector	62%
Total number of medical officers (MCHFP) under the family planning directorate	540
Total number of registered nurses in the country	22,803
Estimated total number of nurses currently available	15,023
Total number of dental surgeons	2995
Total number of family planning officer (TFPO)	546
Total number of assistant family planning officer (ATFPO)	339
Total number of registered medical technologists produced up to 2002 (a) Sanitary inspector (b) Dentists (c) Laboratory technicians (d) Pharmacists (e) Radiographers (f) Physical therapists	952 454 2220 7622 1054 139
Number of medical assistants	5598
Total number of health assistants (HAs) (sanctioned)	21016
Total number of assistant health inspector (sanctioned)	4202
Number of family welfare visitors	5248
Number of health inspectors	1401
Number of family planning inspectors	4110
Total number of family welfare assistants (in position)	22,350

Source Human Resource Development (HRD) Unit, Ministry of Health and Family Welfare, www.mohfwbdgov.org

production, employment and living condition, significantly manipulate the health of the population. Many health policies and programs are doomed to fail due to the lack of resources (Perkins and Roemer 1991). Due to scarce resources, there exist large differences in the access to health care between rich and poor of the poor countries such as Bangladesh (Hjortsberg and Mwikisa 2002). The people of the country must resort either to the government-paid sector of the healthcare system that is often badly equipped and performs poorly in terms of quality of care or to the private healers who provide health services at higher price and sometimes with questionable quality.

There are also other reasons for the backwardness of the public hospitals. These are, for example, lack of empathy, uncaring and casual conduct, aggressive pursuit of monetary gains, poor competence, etc., of the service providers. All these failures play a dominant role in shaping patient's negative attitudes and dissatisfaction with

Table 3.4 Selected indicators of health financing in Bangladesh, 2003

Indicators	Value (%)
Total expenditure on health as percent of GDP	3.2
Total per capita spending in average exchange rate US $	12.0
Public health spending as percent of total	44.2
Public health spending as percent of government budget	8.7
External resources as percent of total public health expenditure	13.3
Private health spending as percent of total	55.88
Out of pocket expenses as percent of total private spending	9.3

Source World Bank (2005)

Table 3.5 Suggested norms for health personnel in Bangladesh

Category of personnel	Norms suggested
Doctors	1 per 3500 population
Nurses	1 per 5000 population
Health worker (male and female)	1 per 5000 population in plain area and 3000 population in tribal and hilly areas
Trained Dai (midwives)	One for each village
Pharmacists	1 per 10,000 population
Laboratory technician	1 per 10,000 population

Source Human Resource Development (HRD) Unit, Ministry of Health and Family Welfare, www.mohfwbdgov.org

healthcare service providers and health care itself (Andaleeb et al. 2007). Besides, economic and sociocultural factors affect the health policy environment of the country. These factors also influence the sociopolitical behavior of the people and the flow of resources for health development of health sector (Johansson et al. 2001) (Tables 3.4 and 3.5).

Like many other developing countries, the public health sector of Bangladesh is plagued by irregular demand and perceptions of poor quality. One study observed that the overall public healthcare services have been declining between 1999 and 2003, while the rate of utilization of private healthcare facilities for the same period has been increasing (Andaleeb et al. 2007). Another recent study demonstrates that the overall utilization rate for public healthcare services of the country is as low as 30% (Ricardo et al. 2004).

The healthcare system of Bangladesh is dominated by the public sector, in terms of both the health services infrastructure, consisting essentially of hospitals, and financing. About 90% of beds are found in public health facilities throughout the country (MOHFW 2005). The density of human resources for health under SAARC region in different years is also quite low in Bangladesh, and it is much low for Bangladesh (WHO 2006). The total number of hospital beds in Bangladesh was

43,293 in 1999, which has increased to 51,684 in 2005. In 2005, 3.43 beds per 10,000 populations were available (U. N. no date).

The value chain of healthcare system of the country is a typical reflection of the underdeveloped country. Figure 3.1 also shows the healthcare value chain of Bangladesh which is actually a strappingly connected system among payers, fiscal intermediaries, service providers, purchasers and producers. It may be observed that governmental authorities or people play the role of the payers, producers are drug/device manufacturers, wholesalers are purchasers, hospitals are service providers and third-party administrators are considered as fiscal intermediaries. This is a typical value chain system of the underdeveloped countries, for example, Bangladesh, India and Pakistan.

Trade in Health Services in Bangladesh

The service sector is the largest contributor to Bangladesh's real GDP growth. This sector grew by 6.47 during the year 2005–2006 compared to 6.36% in 2004–2005 and contributed 49.22% to GDP growth[1]. An analysis of the real growth in GDP achieved in fiscal year (FY) 2008 reveals that service sector contributed 51.2% of the incremental GDP, while industry and agriculture sectors contributed 31.5% and 12.0%, respectively (CPD 2008). All sub-sectors of Bangladesh are shared in the overall growth of the services sector activities, but relatively higher growth rates were registered in education (7.98%), transport, storage and communication (8.25%), hotels and restaurant (7.45%), financial services (7.12%), public administration and defense (8.21%), wholesale and retail trade (7.26%) and health and social work (7.17%).[2]

Trade in health services of Bangladesh, more specifically Bangladesh's import of health services, constitutes an important segment in total bilateral trade between Bangladesh and neighboring countries (Rahman, *op cit*). The available health services data on payments and receipts collected by the Bangladesh Bank in different years show that receipts were low in most of the years, and net medical services show negative figures for fiscal year (FY) 2003–2007 (Table 3.16 and also see A.10). Strikingly, FY 2009 depicts a positive balance (net medical services) and this provides a positive indication of the growth in health trade for the year (Table 3.16).

A large number of Bangladeshi patients are going to foreign hospitals, despite the financial costs and the cumbersome process involved in visas, obtaining foreign exchange, arranging transportation, accommodation, food and locating right health service providers (*Rahman, op cit*). From neighboring countries' perspectives (e.g., India), Bangladesh is a country with high service seeking potential.

---

[1]www.epb.gov.bd.

[2]http://www.epb.gov.bd/bangladesh_country_profile.html.

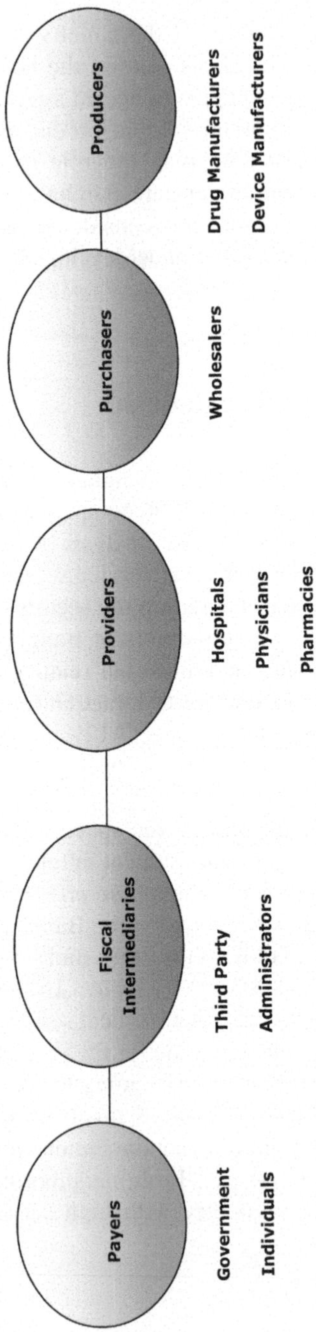

Fig. 3.1 Healthcare value chain in Bangladesh. Adapted from Burns et al. (2002)

Table 3.6 Medical services trade in Bangladesh (value unit in US $)

	FY 2003	FY 04	FY 05	FY 06	FY 07	FY 08
Invisible receipts	0	9823	39,924	10,309	11,219	1,734,875
Invisible payments	522,745	588,712	603,834	429,881	251,044	480,859
Net medical services	−522,745	−578,889	−563,910	−419,572	−239,825	1,254,016

Source Database, Statistics Department, Bangladesh Bank (2009)

Bangladesh mainly imports health services from foreign countries. A large number of Bangladeshi patient seek medical services in foreign countries such as India, Thailand and Singapore.

A study has observed that about 500 million takas (71.2 million US $) is spent by the Bangladeshi patients each year to avail treatment in foreign hospitals (IHE 2002). Bangladesh's trade in health services actually is dominated with import of services from foreign countries (Table 3.6).

There is a dearth of reliable data or information on imports of health services in Bangladesh (Rahman, *op cit*). There are no reliable data on such important indicators like number of individuals seeking services in India, reasons for the import of such services, modes of payments, structure of expenditures and quantum of foreign exchange spent, etc. The lack of data actually hinders adequate understanding of the state, scope and dynamics of this type of trade among countries under the SAARC region and other foreign countries.

Table 3.7 depicts that although a substantial number of service trade-related requests have been made by several countries, to date no country has made any request to Bangladesh to liberalize its health and social service sector under the GATS mode. It reveals that a relatively large number of requests were made for telecommunication services, financial services, business services and transport services (Table 3.7).

Health Service Trade in Bangladesh Under Four Modes: Potentials and Barriers

Cross-border Supply of Trade (Telemedicine, Mode 1)

Cross-border supply of trade does not involve the physical movement of the supplier or consumer. Trade through electronic means as also border crossing by material substances that embody services in them would fall under this mode. Telemedicine is an example of health service trade where physical movement of the supplier and consumer is not needed. Telemedicine can be broadly defined as the use of information technology to provide patient care and share clinical information from one

Table 3.7 Request to Bangladesh at sub-sector levels

	Service sub-sectors	Total sub-sectors	Requests made	Number of requesting countries	Major requesting countries
1. Business services		46	35	5	USA, EC
	1A. Professional services	11	10	3	USA
	1B. Computer and related services	5	5	2	EC
	1C. Research and development services	3	0	0	
	1D. Real estate services	2	0	0	
	1E. Rental/leasing services without operators	5	0	0	
	1F. Other business services	20	20	3	EC, USA
2. Communication services		28	23	6	USA, EC, Japan, Norway
	2A. Postal services	1	0		
	2B. Courier services	1	1	1	USA
	2C. Telecommunication services	20	20	6	USA, EC, Japan, Norway
	2D. Audiovisual services	6	2		
3. Construction and related engineering services		5	5	3	Japan, EC
4. Distribution services		5	5	2	Japan, USA
5. Educational services		5	0	0	
6. Environmental services		4	4	3	USA, EC, Norway
7. Financial services		17	17		
	7A. All insurance and insurance-related services	4	4	5	USA, EC, Japan
	7B. Banking and other financial services	12	12	5	USA, EC, Japan

(continued)

Table 3.7 (continued)

	Service sub-sectors	Total sub-sectors	Requests made	Number of requesting countries	Major requesting countries
	7C. Other	1	1	5	USA, EC, Japan
8. Health-related and social services		4	0	0	
9. Tourism and travel-related services		4	1	1	
	9A. Hotels and restaurants (including catering)	1	1	1	
	9B. Travel agencies and tour operator services	1	0	0	
	9C. Tourist guide services	1	0	0	
	9D. Other	1	0	0	
10. Recreational, cultural and sporting services		5	1	1	
	10A. Entertainment services	1	1	1	
	10B. News agency services	1	0	0	
	10C. Libraries, archives, museums and other cultural services	1	0	0	
	10D. Sporting and other recreational services	1	0	0	
	10E. Other	1	0	0	
11. Transport services		35	35	4	Japan, EC
	11A. Maritime transport services	6	6	4	Japan, EC
	11B. Internal waterways transport	6	6	2	Japan
	11C. Air transport services	5	5	2	Japan
	11D. Space transport	1	1	1	Japan
	11E. Rail transport services	5	5	1	Japan

(continued)

Table 3.7 (continued)

	Service sub-sectors	Total sub-sectors	Requests made	Number of requesting countries	Major requesting countries
	11F. Road transport services	5	5	1	Japan
	11G. Pipeline transport	2	2	1	Japan
	11H. Services auxiliary to all modes of transport	4	4	4	Japan, EC
	11I. Other transport services	1	1	3	Japan
12. Other services not included				1	USA
Horizontal	Development of e-commerce	1	1	1	USA
	Mode 4	1	1	6	Japan, USA, EC, Norway

Source Raihan (2005)

geographic location to another. The use of telemedicine brings about changes in health care and opens up new possibilities in service delivery for the underdeveloped countries. Telemedicine involves several possible services provided synchronously in real time or asynchronously at a later time (Rafiq et al. 2005).

Some studies opine that telemedicine divides the world into those who have access to 'real doctors' and face-to-face care, and others who remain contended with electronically mediated and sensorial anesthetized relationships (Nicolini 2006). A question is often asked: 'will physicians exhibit the same degree of 'care' for those patients who receive distant treatment?' (Cartwright 2000, p. 257). This type of question is raised by the researcher to question about the effectiveness of telemedicine service in medical treatment.

Although the pitfalls of this type of mode service are sometimes mentioned, several studies have noted the benefit of using telemedicine in health care, especially in the poor countries (Broens et al. 2007; Hjelm 2005; Johnston et al. 2004; Rafiq et al. 2007). It has been observed that telemedicine reduces costs substantially (Rafiq, et al. 2007). Cross-border delivery of health services through telemedicine can enable healthcare providers to cater to remote and underserved segments of the population (Chanda 2002). This can be done with the help of electronic delivery of health services, such as telediagnostics, surveillance and consultation services, telepathology and teleradiology (e.g., India to Bangladesh and Nepal) and e-health (products and services available over Internet).

It is often noted that telemedicine helps to alleviate some human resource constraints, enable more cost-effective surveillance of diseases, improve quality of diagnosis and treatment, upgrade skills, etc (Hjelm 2005; Johnston et al. 2004). The impact that telemedicine can have on the healthcare system is entirely dependent on the degree of integration. With the network of technologies and human factors, telemedicine provides cost reductions in the delivery of health care and facilitates consultations without respect to state or national borders.

A recent study has noted that healthcare needs of underserved poor countries in Africa can be effectively addressed, with the establishment of a telemedicine network, using community hospital in an industrialized country, e.g., in France (Johnston et al. 2004). In this type of service, physicians are linked to each other through virtual network within the Internet where they are readily available to collaborate in a requested role from a distant site. The skilled health professionals of the developing countries have the potential to provide consultation from a distance. Currently, medical images such as X-rays, MRI images and other types of medical images can be digitized and transmitted via computer and Internet from one country to another.

Telemedicine Service in Bangladesh

There are several telemedicine service providers in Bangladesh, a few of them are working at the cross-border level (A-IV), these are mainly private-level initiatives, and they mainly import telemedicine services from foreign countries. Some of these healthcare providers give services at both the domestic and international levels. A study, after analyzing some telemedicine projects and their activities, opines that Bangladesh has much potential in telemedicine services (Nessa et al. 2008). This study, after reviewing existing functions of the service providers, proposed a prototype telemedicine network for Bangladesh.

One of the largest telemedicine service providers in the country is Medinova Telemedicine. This is a project of the Medinova Health Care based in the capital city of Dhaka. Through this service, a private hospital like Medinova is connected with super-speciality hospitals in India like AIIMS in New Delhi, Apollo Hospital in Madras, Sankara Nethralaya, Max Cardiac Hospital, Kranti Kidney Hospital in Kerala and CARE in Hyderabad (A-IV). The facility of the services allows tele-consultation and videoconferencing between Bangladeshi doctors with specialists in India.

There are also several other telemedicine service providers in the country, and these hospitals and private organizations import most of their services from India, East Asian countries and North America. In the private sector, telemedicine is expected to make up for the shortfall in specialized human resources in certain hospital facilities.

Cross-border Supply of Trade (Telemedicine) in Bangladesh: Opportunities and Barriers

It has been gathered through field study that Bangladesh has potential for health service imports and exports through Mode 1. Telemedicine has the potential to deliver health services to countries under the SAARC region using the state-of-the-art technology. It may also be considered as an opportunity for economic development of the country. Bangladeshi hospitals can provide best possible treatment to their patients through telemedicine. Telemedicine discourages movement of the Bangladeshi patients to foreign land as they can receive the medical services from foreign doctors without moving to a foreign land and check illegal (unreported) money transactions which are mostly carried through informal channels with India and other foreign countries (Rahman, *op cit*). The implementation and use of this technology may be a tool to stop huge amount of illegal foreign exchange outflow from the country each year.

A recent study estimates that there are 1.1 million PCs in the country (7.3 PCs per 1000 population) (UNDP 2008, quoted in DGHS 2008). With the Bangladesh's accession to the WTO service sector like telecommunications, insurance, banking etc. are being liberalized and progressively opened up (A-V). The liberalization steps in telecommunication sector may have a significant and positive affect on telemedicine services at the cross-border level which actually depends heavily on the liberalization of telecommunications, information and communication technology (ICT).

Some service providers opined that several factors hinder the implementation process of telemedicine services in Bangladesh (A-IV). Resistance from doctors who feel threatened by alternative approaches, high initial expense of setting up some telemedicine systems, difficulty in justifying high costs, reimbursing insurance, legal liability issue, etc., hinders the process of the development and implementation of telemedicine services in the country. Another barrier is the lack of privacy and security regulations. Telemedicine is capital intensive, and there exists possible diversion of resources from basic preventive and curative services. This service may also impair equity if it caters to a small section of the population, for example only urban affluent of the country. Besides, most patients still prefer to see their physicians so the trust in the accuracy of findings generated through telemedicine needs to be built up (Dacanay and Rodolfo 2005). Partnering between a local healthcare provider and a reputable institution in the target market may help overcome this barrier.

Telemedicine may have also some detrimental effect if its basic aspects are not considered while implementing this service mode. Incompatible information infrastructure, poor diagnostic and imaging studies, and weak hospital infrastructure may hinder the development of telemedicine services in Bangladesh. Telemedicine may create obstacle in resolving the cases about malpractice liability and coverage (Rafiq et al. 2005).

Although health service trade through Mode 1 has much potential for Bangladesh, it is observed from field study that poor computer literacy among physicians, low technical expertise, lack of motivation and interest, technology phobia and lack of initiatives from the government hinder the development and expansion of telemedicine services in Bangladesh (A-IV).

Consumption Abroad (Mode 2)

It can be here mentioned that healthcare service providers and planners in Bangladesh are often more concerned about the cost of health care rather than its quality. There exists a general feeling among Bangladeshi healthcare provider that people do not want to pay more for higher service quality. This is not correct in reality. A large number of patients avail private healthcare services within the country and also from foreign hospitals.

To identify reasons for the import of health services by Bangladeshi patients, costs in treatment among domestic private and public hospitals and foreign hospitals are compared. The cost of treatment of seven diseases (coronary bypass graft surgery, breast lump removal, knee joint replacement, lasik surgery, cataract surgery, in vitro fertilization (IVF) cycle and hernia correction) is compared among USA, UK, Singapore, India and Bangladesh (Table 3.17 and Fig. 3.2). The data for cost of treatment from both private and public hospitals in Bangladesh have been collected through field survey and compared with published data of the four other countries (Table 3.8).

The findings of the comparison (Tables 3.17, 3.19 and 3.20) indicate that although the cost of treatment is low in Bangladesh (in both public and private hospitals), patients of the country are ready to pay higher price for treatment in the foreign hospitals and due to this a large number of patients receive health services from India and other foreign countries. The Confederation of Indian Industry and McKinsey

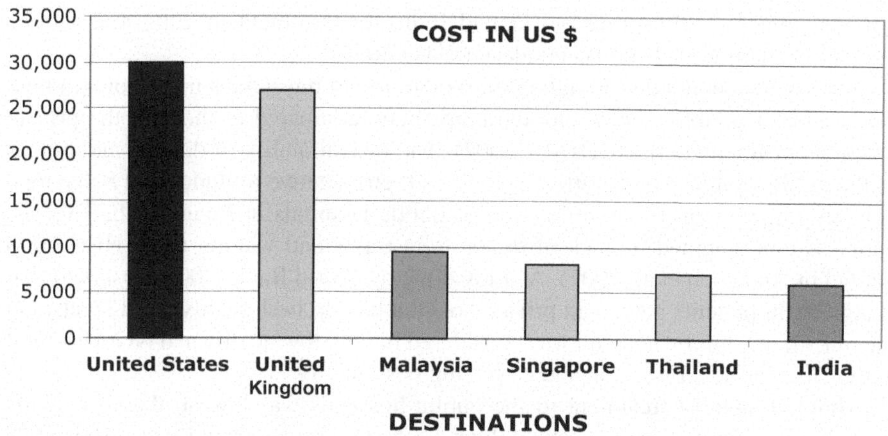

Fig. 3.2 Global cost differences for cardiac surgery. *Source* http://www.sitacare.com/

Table 3.8 Comparative costs of treatment (USA, UK, Singapore, India and Bangladesh, in US $)

	USA	UK (private hospital)	Singapore	India	Bangladesh (government hospital)	Bangladesh (private hospital)
Coronary bypass graft surgery	35,000	25,000	–	6000	1324 (full package)	3221
Breast lump removal	–	3200	1000	700	41 (medicine should be bought by the patient)	441
Knee joint replacement	–	15,000	7000	5000	1912 (only instrument, no operation cost)	3088
Lasik surgery	4000	2800	1600	700	–	–
No stitch cataract surgery	4500	2600	–	700	59 (medicine and lenses should be bought by the patient)	588
In vitro fertilization (IVF) cycle	15,000	–	–	1800	–	1647
Hernia correction	2800	2700	2500	1000	41 (medicine should be bought by the patient)	500

Source http://www.indianhealthguru.com/price-cost-surgery-india.htm and Field Survey (2009)

reported that 150,000 foreigners visited India for treatment in 2004 and a large number of them were from Bangladesh (WTO 2007).

A study also noted that Bangladeshi patient found physicians in the foreign hospitals more available, competent and empathetic compared to those in the private hospitals in Bangladesh (ICDDRB 2007). The unavailability of doctors and nurses in the public healthcare facilities, as well as their negative attitudes and behaviors, is a key impediment to the utilization of public hospitals in Bangladesh. This situation is compounded by lack of drugs, long travel and waiting time (HEU 2003 quoted in Andaleeb et al. 2007). A study done by World Bank (2005) observed that Bangladeshi patients perceived private hospital having best quality at all levels. On the other hand, public hospital was considered having low quality and NGO hospital at the Upazila[3] level was considered having best quality.

Although cost of treatment in the public hospitals was lowest, these hospitals provide poor quality services (World Bank 2005). On the other hand, private hospitals

[3] Administrative unit like police station.

were more costly but their services were considered more improved. The Government of Bangladesh and non-government organizations (NGOs) have also acknowledged their concern about the overall healthcare services of the country (World Bank 2003) (Tables 3.9 and 3.10).

It is observed that an increasing number of foreign patients are going to India for treatment from developing and also to some developed countries. Bangladeshi patients perceive foreign healthcare services to be more reasonably priced (ICDDRB 2007). Relatively better and low-cost treatment in India and proximity are principal reasons for patients going to India from neighboring countries such as Sri Lanka, Bangladesh and Nepal. A large part of transactions for trade in health services for Bangladesh, for example, goes unreported (especially in case of India) since such transactions are carried mostly through informal channels and therefore not reflected in the balance of payment accounts. It can be observed that countries like Thailand, Singapore and Malaysia which belong to the ASEAN region earn huge amount of foreign exchange from their neighboring countries (Table 3.11) through health

Table 3.9 Export of health tourism services by three countries in the ASEAN region

Country	Export revenues	Number of patients	Origin of patients
Malaysia (2003)	US $40 million	More than 100,000	60% from Indonesia and 10% from other ASEAN countries
Singapore (2002)	US $420 million	210,000	45% from Indonesia, 20% from Malaysia, 3% from other ASEAN countries
Thailand	US $482 million	470,000 (2001) 630,000 (2002)	42% from the Far East (mostly Japan) and 7% from ASEAN countries

Sources Arunanondchai and Carsten (2006)

Table 3.10 Cost of treatment in Bangladesh, cardiac intervention

Types of intervention	Government hospitals	Private hospitals
(a1) Cost of ring operation/stunting (including accommodation for 3–5 days) (a2) Price of ring	(a1) US $217–289 (a2) US $434–1449 (Ordinary)	(a1) US $580–797 (a2) Drug eluting special type of ring (long lasting) US $2898–3333
(b) Balloon valve plasty (including 3 days accommodation costs)	(b) US $217–261	(b) US $289–725
(c) Pacemaker fixing (permanent) including cost of pacemaker (1 piece) and accommodation and other costs	(c) US $217–362	(c) US $435–724

Source Shaptahik (2006) (www.shaptahik2000.com)

Table 3.11 Ordinal degrees and cardinal weights

Ordinal degree	Cardinal weight
I (1st)	1
II (2nd)	2
III (3rd)	3
IV (4th)	4
V (5th)	5
VI (6th)	6
VII (7th)	7
.	.
.	.
XVII (17th)	17

service trading and this may be a good example for Bangladesh and other South Asian countries, e.g., India, Nepal, Bhutan and Pakistan. Bangladesh also can earn huge amount of foreign exchange if it can develop its health infrastructure. An effective and sound health policy is needed in this respect.

Healthcare Seeking Behavior of the Bangladeshi Patients: An Application of Mean Score of Relative Importance (MSRI) Method

To analyze the relative importance of the factors which motivated Bangladeshi patients to seek services from various types of hospitals mentioned before, Mean Score of Relative Importance (MSRI) analysis was carried out (A-IV). MSRI technique, which is a descriptive statistical technique, was administered to analyze data. The formula of MSRI is given below (Huque 2001).

$$\text{MSRI} = \frac{\sum W_i + (n - f)N}{n}$$

where

ΣW_i is the total sum of cardinal weights assigned to different degrees of importance for the factor in question pointed out by the respondents.
n is the total size of sample.
f is the total number of respondents pointed out the factor in question (i.e., the frequency of the factor).
N is the total number of factors contributing to satisfaction (or dissatisfaction).

Firstly, ordinal weights were assigned to different degrees of importance indicated by the respondents. Afterward, the cardinal weights were assigned to different degrees of importance to calculate Mean Score of Relative Importance (Table 3.21). The formula used in the present study is more robust than a simple weighted average method (Alam 1986; Huque 2001).

The study sees the health-related service factors from service quality (service quality or SERVQUAL) point of view. Parasuraman et al. (1988), and Zeithaml and Bitner (2006) note that there are five dimensions of consumer's service quality judgment when marketing perspectives are taken into consideration. These dimensions are (a) reliability, (b) responsiveness, (c) assurance, (d) empathy and (e) tangibles. These dimensions are discussed below.

Reliability

Reliability is defined as the ability to perform the promised service dependably and accurately. In the broadest sense, reliability emphasizes promises about delivery of services, problem resolution ability and pricing and other core service attributes of the company.

Responsiveness

Responsiveness is the willingness to help customers and to provide prompt service. This dimension emphasizes attentiveness and promptness in dealing with customer requests, questions, complaints and problems.

Assurance

Assurance is defined as employees' knowledge and courtesy and the ability of the firm and its employees to inspire trust and confidence.

Empathy

Empathy is defined as the caring, individualized attention the firm provides its customers. The essence of empathy is conveying, through personalized or customized service, that customers are unique and special.

Tangibles

Tangibles are defined as the appearance of physical facilities, equipment, personnel and communication materials. All of these provide physical representations or images of the service that customers, particularly new customers, will use to evaluate quality.

Total of 26 health service factors were classified according to SERVQUAL dimensions. The classification of these factors is given in Table 3.23. Table 3.24 depicts the consolidated MSRI results of the three types of hospitals. These are government hospitals, private hospitals in Bangladesh and hospitals located in India (coded as BD_Govt_MSRI, BD_Private_MSRI and INDIA_MSRI) (Table 3.12).

Table 3.12 Hospital-related service factors and dimension of SERVQUAL

Hospital-related service factors	SERVQUAL dimension
F1. Competency of the doctors	Reliability
F2. Competency of the nurses	Reliability
F3. Pathological laboratory equipped with all kinds of testing facilities	Tangible
F4. Waiting time to get appointment is short	Responsiveness
F5. Low treatment cost of the hospital	Reliability/cost
F6. Hospital is visually appealing	Tangibles
F7. Ambulance facility	Tangibles
F8. Hospitals have modern medical equipments	Tangibles
F9. Good-quality food	Tangibles
F10. Accommodation cost low	Reliability/cost
F11. Specialist doctors are available	Reliability
F12. Hospital staffs respond promptly when needed	Responsiveness
F13. Follow-up treatment is good	Empathy
F14. Doctors listen to one's problem attentively	Assurance
F15. Nurses are very caring and willing to respond when needed	Assurance
F16. Easy to get bed/cabin in the hospital	Assurance
F17. Non-repetitive pathological test	Assurance

Analysis of the MSRI Result: Patients from Government Hospitals in Bangladesh

It can be seen from the tables that patients ranked competency of the doctor and availability of specialist doctors as their prime reasons (Rank 1) for visiting government hospitals. Patients who visited government hospitals ranked low-cost treatment with 2 and short waiting time with 3. Government hospitals are always the last resort for the poor patients for low-cost treatment. These attitudes of the patients can be examined from service quality perspectives. It seems that reliability, responsiveness and cost of treatment were the prime motivating factors behind selecting government hospitals. Patients of the government hospitals did not judge quality of food (F9) as an important factor in choosing these hospitals. They, in fact, did not consider repetitive pathological test (F17) as an important factor for selecting the hospitals (Table 3.13).

Table 3.13 Comparative analysis of MSRI

Name	F1	F2	F3	F4	F5	F6	F7	F8	F9	F10	F11	F12	F13	F14	F15	F16	F17
BD_Govt_MSRI	2.67	7.75	7.50	4.67	4.50	8.83	9.67	4.92	12.75	4.83	2.00	5.42	6.58	5.92	7.33	6.58	13.50
BD_Private_MSRI	1.43	4.79	4.71	3.14	7.43	10.14	14.29	4.29	14.79	10.71	2.57	5.93	4.79	2.71	5.36	7.07	11.07
INDIA_MSRI	1.75	4.44	5.00	15.44	13.63	10.25	16.63	5.38	16.31	16.31	1.81	3.44	1.81	2.63	3.19	16.56	5.31

Analysis of MSRI Result: Patients from Private Hospitals in Bangladesh

Competency of specialist doctors (F1) was the most important criterion for the patients to select private hospitals in Bangladesh. The patient identified those specialist doctors (F11) who used to listen to the problems of the patients (F14) with care. It was the second most important decisive factor to select private hospitals. Reliability and assurance dimensions were also important service quality aspects that motivated patients to receive services from private hospitals. Short waiting time to receive appointment was the third most important criterion to decide on the private hospitals.

It can be observed from Table 3.23 that 'relative waiting time to see the doctor' is high in case of private hospitals when compared with government hospitals. It seems that there were some tangible elements (modern equipment or F8, and good pathological facilities or F3) which actually attracted patients to choose private hospitals. Like government hospitals, quality of food (F9) did have any important bearing on selecting private hospitals.

Analysis of MSRI Result: Patients from Hospitals in India

The cost factor (F5) had low level of significance for the patients, who visited India to receive treatment (Table 3.23). Bangladeshi patients had to wait long for getting doctors' appointment (F4), but finally received reliable treatment with high levels of assurance and empathy. Most of the patients selected Indian hospitals, as specialist doctors were available there (F11) and they had high level of competency (F1). In addition to this, most of the patients visited India, as these hospitals provided good follow-up treatment (F13). Indian doctors listened to the patients' problems with care (F14), and this was the second most important decisive factor for selecting treatment in India (Table 3.24). Prompt and good nursing services were also important determinants which allured the patients to choose Indian hospitals. Patients, who selected India as their destination for treatment, did not bother much about the accommodation cost (F10) and quality of food (F9) (Tables 3.14 and 3.15).

Consumption Abroad: Opportunities and Risks

The specific nature of health consumption generates barriers to patients' mobility. The psychological cost of going abroad can be high for the patient. It is not the consumer's choice that always defines the nature, scope, etc., of the health service consumption but also the physician's instructions. The problem of follow-up and

Table 3.14 Service quality factors, MSRI ranking and SERVQUAL dimensions

Type of hospitals	Factors		Weight	SERVQUAL	Rank
Government hospitals, Bangladesh	Specialist doctors available	F11	2.00	Reliability	Rank 1
	Competency of doctors	F1	2.67	Reliability	
	Low treatment cost of the hospital	F5	4.50	Reliability/cost	Rank 2
	Waiting time to get appointment is short	F4	4.67	Responsiveness	
	Accommodation cost is low	F10	4.83	Reliability/cost	Rank 3
	Hospital has modern medical equipments	F8	4.92	Tangibles	
	Hospital staffs respond promptly when needed	F12	5.42	Responsiveness	Rank 4
Private hospitals, Bangladesh	Competency of the doctors	F1	1.43	Reliability	Rank 1
	Specialist doctors are available	F11	2.57	Reliability	Rank 2
	Doctors listen to one's problem attentively	F14	2.71	Assurance	
	Waiting time to get appointment is short	F4	3.14	Responsiveness	Rank 3
	Hospital has modern medical equipments	F8	4.29	Tangibles	Rank 4
	Pathological facilities equipped with all types of testing facilities	F3	4.71	Tangibles	Rank 5
	Competency of nurses	F2	4.79	Reliability	
	Follow-up treatment is good	F13	4.79	Empathy	
Hospitals in India	Competency of the doctors	F1	1.75	Reliability	Rank 1
	Specialist doctors are available	F11	1.81	Reliability	
	Follow-up treatment is good	F13	1.81	Empathy	

(continued)

Table 3.14 (continued)

Type of hospitals	Factors		Weight	SERVQUAL	Rank
	Doctors listen to one's problem attentively	F14	2.63	Assurance	Rank 2
	Nurses are very caring and willing to respond when needed	F15	3.19	Assurance	Rank 3
	Hospital staffs respond promptly when needed	F12	3.44	Responsiveness	
	Competency of nurses	F2	4.44	Reliability	Rank 4

Table 3.15 Identified strength and weaknesses of the public, private and NGO health service providers in Bangladesh

Type of services	Cost	Perceived quality	Technical quality	Subjective performance	Accessibility	Price
Public	Lowest costs found at the national level Highest costs found at the district level	Lowest perceived quality scores	Slightly lower technical quality than private facilities, increasing with level			Lowest prices at all levels
Private	Lowest costs found at the district level Highest costs found at the national level	Best perceived quality scores at all levels	Technical quality increasing with level		High levels have higher accessibility scores from the facility's standpoint, but lower scores from the patient's standpoint	Highest prices at all levels, increasing with the level of attention
NGO	Shows a similar cost than private and public facilities at the Upazila (small administrative unit) level	Best perceived quality scores at the Upazila (administrative unit) level	Best technical quality scores	Best subjective performance scores	Have the highest accessibility score from the patient's standpoint	Low prices

Source World Bank (2005)

aftercare when the patient is back home increases considerably the cost (and the risk) of this type of international transaction.

The opportunities involved with consumption abroad may be listed below:

- For exporting countries like India, consumption abroad generates foreign exchange earnings and increases resources for health service.
- It helps the exporting countries to upgrade its health infrastructure and knowledge about health service.
- Bangladeshi patients receive quality treatment.
- This type of service helps Bangladesh to overcome the shortages of physical and human resources in the specialty areas.
- It provides incentives to the local entrepreneurs to establish joint venture hospitals with modern and world-class equipments and facilities in the importing countries like Bangladesh. These may attract local patients to receive services in these hospitals. A tendency of establishing modern hospitals can already be seen in the country (e.g., Apollo Hospital, United Hospital, Square Hospital, etc.).
- Bangladesh can promote Mode 2 to export health services by adopting some strategies. The strategies may be: (a) establishing excellence in specialist areas; (b) giving health tourism package; (c) investing more resources in modern medical equipments; and (d) encouraging referrals, etc. These strategies may attract patients living specially in eastern part of India and Myanmar to receive services from modern private hospitals in Bangladesh.

There are also some risks associated with this mode of health service for importing countries like Bangladesh. These are:

- It will crowd out poor domestic population. This is particularly true for Bangladesh, where a large number of people remain outside periphery of the modern and relatively costly treatment provided by the hospitals of the foreign countries.
- There is no doubt that a huge amount of foreign exchange of Bangladesh will outflow to foreign countries, often through illegal way as Bangladeshi patients will spend huge amount of foreign exchange in India and East Asian countries like Thailand and Singapore for receiving treatments by the Bangladeshi patients.

Commercial Presence (Mode 3)

Commercial presence (Mode 3) involves the establishment of healthcare providers or firms in the healthcare sector outside their home nation through foreign direct investment (FDI) in equity or non-equity forms. The common pattern of foreign participation (mainly hospitals and specialized clinics) is to invest in existing facilities or enter a joint venture with local partners (Outreville 2007). Inflow of foreign capital provides additional resources to invest in the healthcare infrastructures and services of the country.

Table 3.16 Ease of doing business ranking (selected)

Rank	Country
1	Canada
11	Singapore
30	Mauritius
40	Kazakhstan
68	Bangladesh
79	Bhutan
88	India
97	Vietnam
128	China
159	Cambodia

Source World Bank (2007)

The most direct beneficiaries in this respect are people who can afford the services offered by foreign suppliers. The benefits go beyond the direct impact for patients receiving the services from the foreign providers and can have system-wide impacts. They can take the form of access to new technologies and services, information, management techniques (Blouin 2006). It has been observed that FDI in services exceeds manufacturing and this tendency concerns both developed and developing countries (OECD 2005).

A study has shown that doing business in Bangladesh today is easier than many developing economies (Table 3.16). A report entitled '*Doing Business in 2007: Creating Jobs*' published jointly by the World Bank and IFC ranked Bangladesh in the 68th position in terms of starting a business and ease of doing business among 175 economies (Table 3.16).

In the above ranking based on ten categories, Bangladesh appears as one of the easiest locations for doing business in South Asia. Government of Bangladesh has undertaken a long-term Private Sector Development Support Project (PSDSP) to improve the investment climate of the country. The main components of the project are reforming the business-related regulatory framework and focusing on the establishment of special economic zone and capacity building of the related agencies.[4]

Foreign Direct Investment (FDI) in Service Sector of Bangladesh

It can be observed that a recent shift in FDI has been toward services. Table 28 depicts the FDI inflow (including that in export processing zones, EPZs) over the last 11 years. With the country's accession to the World Trade Organization (WTO),

[4]http://www.boi.gov.bd/boi_services.php.

service sectors like power and energy, banking, insurance and telecommunications are being liberalized and progressively opened up. The sector-wise inflow of FDI during 1998–2007 is presented in Table 3.17. There are three broad sectors of FDI inflows: infrastructure, manufacturing and services. The shares of the three sectors are 46%, 27% and 27%, respectively (Fig. 3.3).

FDI has significant impact on the economy of Bangladesh. Bhattcharaya and Dev (2004) estimated that a 10% investment in Bangladesh might increase GDP up to 3.71% and it was estimated that about 13% increase in the foreign investment was necessary to reduce about 1% level of poverty.

The rate of foreign investment in Bangladesh from the South Asian countries is very meager. The total investment made by the countries under the South Asian region was less than 2–3% of the total investment made in the country (Bhattacharya 2002). If we look at Table 3.18, it can be observed that only India plays a somewhat significant role among the SAARC countries. In the year 2006, India invested US $6.09 million in Bangladesh. The amount comprises about 0.77% of the total investment in Bangladesh. Pakistan, on the other hand, invested US $5.14 million in Bangladesh in 2006. Sri Lanka invested about US $2.63 million. Other countries within the SAARC region had no worth mentioning investment into Bangladesh (Tables 3.17 and 3.18).

Major investments in the country from India were from companies like Asian Paints, Apollo Hospital (a health service investment), Reckitt Benckiser, VIP-Nitol, Mann Pharma, Cello GQ Industries, Berger Paints and Data Soft Ltd (Bhattacharya 2002).

Although doing business is easy in Bangladesh, many foreign investors involved in health service trading find it risky to invest in the developing countries like Bangladesh, where only a few can afford private treatment (Smith 2004). There are a small number of hospitals which have been established under joint ventures in Bangladesh (e.g., Apollo Hospital in Dhaka, a joint project of Apollo Hospital Enterprise Limited and STS Holdings Limited).[5]

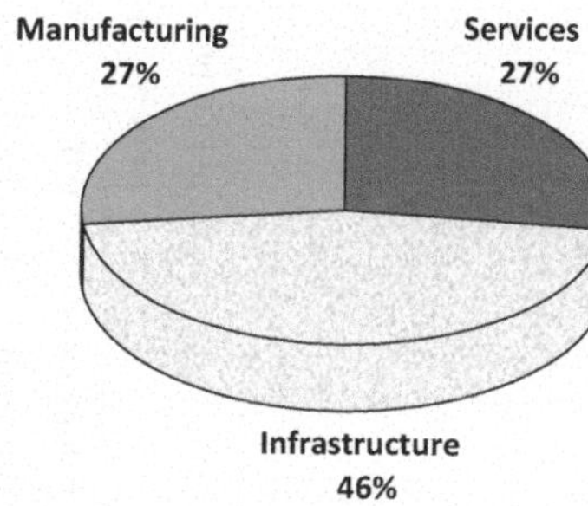

Fig. 3.3 Major sector-wise share of FDI flow

[5]Some of these hospitals are facing problems in recent months. Apollo Hospital, which started its operations in Dhaka with an investment of US $45 million, is to reorganize management after it fails to make substantial profit. Employees of the Apollo Hospital on March 8, 2008, staged demonstrations after 150 members of the staff, including doctors and nurses, were sacked. Apollo

Table 3.17 Aggregate and sector-wise FDI inflow, 1995–2005 (in million US $)

Sectors	1995	1996	1997	1998	1999	2000	2001	2002	2003	2004	2005
Agriculture and fishing (total)	0.0	0.3	1.4	1.4	2.9	15.2	1.1	1.6	4.1	1.7	2.3
Power, gas and petroleum	3.2	47.0	242.1	235.2	83.5	301.0	192.4	57.9	88.1	124.1	208.3
Manufacturing	45.5	89.2	162.4	139.8	191.8	193.5	132.2	142.9	165.2	139.4	219.3
Industry (total)	48.7	136.2	404.5	375	275.3	494.5	324.6	200.8	253.3	263.5	427.6
Trade commerce	41.3	92.3	158.9	164.3	27.5	53.2	27.6	63.7	44.0	66.6	130.5
Transport and telecom	1.7	1.5	5.9	25.3	0.5	5.4	0.9	48.5	45.9	127.5	281.9
Other services	0.6	1.3	4.6	10.5	2.9	10.3	0.3	13.7	2.9	1.1	3.0
Services (total)	43.6	95.1	169.4	200.0	30.9	68.9	28.8	125.9	92.8	195.2	415.4
Total FDI to Bangladesh	92.3	231.6	575.3	576.5	309.1	578.6	354.5	328.3	350.2	460.4	845.0

Source Bangladesh Bank Enterprise Survey

Table 3.18 FDI inflow in Bangladesh from selected countries (in million $US)

FDI source	2005 (total)	2005 (rank)	2006 (total)	2006 (share) (%)	2006 (rank)
India	2.7	18	6.09	0.77	14
Nepal	0.1	30	–	–	–
Pakistan	25.5	12	5.14	0.65	16
Sri Lanka	4.1	17	2.63	0.33	18
Egypt	48.4	7	105.36	13.03	2
Norway	53.5	5	82.95	10.47	4
UAE	55.4	4	88.02	11.11	3
UK	152.8	1	70.47	8.89	5
USA	141.8	2	175.72	22.17	1

Source Bangladesh Bank Enterprise Survey (2007) (www.boi.gov.bd)

Commercial Presence: Opportunities and Barriers

It is anticipated that FDI in health sector will bring additional resources and expertise to improve the range, quality and efficiency of services offered. It is understandable that this depends on regulation that exists. The presence of increased health technology through FDI may encourage the Bangladesh government to invest in such technology, and the government may feel to improve the health service condition of the public sector.

The commercial presence in healthcare services in Bangladesh can generate additional resources for investment in and upgrading of healthcare infrastructure and technologies. Nevertheless, concerns remain about the possible negative effects of FDI, including the question of market power, technological dependence, capital flight and profit outflow. It is also observed that in respect of Mode 3 the services usually non-tradable and an influx of foreign enterprises such as companies from India and East Asian countries (e.g., Thailand and Malaysia) can cause significant outflow of investment income from Bangladesh. This may lead to negative effects on the Bangladesh's balance of payments (Khor 2006).

Hospital of Dhaka is running at only 50% of its capacity as competition heats up at the top end of the private healthcare market in the capital. Apollo was built to provide space for 450 patient beds, but less than 300 are installed. Of these, the hospital is not able to fill more than 155 Square Hospital and United Hospital are among the top end private healthcare facilities in Bangladesh. These hospitals and some other private hospitals are also providing world-class services and are involved in intense competition with foreign hospitals like Apollo, Dhaka (The Daily Star, 13-3-2008).

Temporary Movement of Natural Person (TMNP, Mode 4)

Temporary movement of natural person (TMNP, Mode 4) is defined in Article 1:2 of the GATS as 'Supply of a service… by a service supplier of a member through presence of natural persons of a member in the territory of any other member.' It includes both service providers who are working overseas in an individual capacity and service providers who are part of a home, host or third country commercial establishment (Chanda 2001). GATS also contains a separate annex on the movement of natural persons. The annex defines the scope of Mode 4 to cover 'persons who are temporarily working in another member country. It is not applicable to individuals who are seeking access to the employment market of another member on a permanent basis or for citizenship or residency purposes' (Chanda 2001). Developing countries always stress that political will from the developed countries is needed for a meaningful liberalization of Mode 4, and this mode should be treated as a trade and development issue of the poor countries (Khor, *ibid*).

It is understood that temporary movement of natural persons can play an important role in the economy of Bangladesh in terms of maintaining macroeconomic stability of the country, reduces pressure on the national unemployment, helps poverty alleviation and investment in agriculture, etc. In fiscal year 2007–2008, remittance earnings of the wage earners have increased to US $7914.78 million, and in 2008–2009 it was US $8770.16 (up to the month of May) (Table 3.20). Table 3.19 depicts percentage changes over corresponding period of the previous years, and it may be observed that the changes were quite significant. The number of workers going abroad to provide services is around 23% of the total population entering the labor force (Raihan and Mahmood 2004). It may be mentioned that here that Special Modalities of Negotiations on Service Trade Liberalization for Least Developed Countries (LDCs) which had been adopted on September 3, 2003 on the eve of Cancun Ministerial meeting and this has opened up new opportunities for LDCs to deal with this issues. Article 8 of the Special Modalities mentioned: 'It is recognized that the temporary movement of natural persons supplying services (Mode 4) provides potential benefits to the sending and recipient members. LDCs have indicated that this is one of the most important means of supplying services internationally. Members shall, to the extent possible, and consistently with Article XIX of the GATS consider undertaking commitments to provide access in Mode 4, taking into account all categories of natural persons identified by LDCs in their requests' (Tables 3.19 and 3.20).

Table 3.19 Annual trends in remittances

Year	Million US $
2005–2006	4801.88 (+243.47)
2006–2007	5978.47 (+24.50)
2007–2008	7914.78 (+32.39)

Source Foreign Exchange Policy Department, Bangladesh Bank
Note Figures in brackets indicate percentage changes over the corresponding period of the previous year

Table 3.20 Wage earners' remittance inflows (yearly)

Year	Million US $
2008–2009*	8770.16
2007–2008	7914.78
2006–2007	5998.47
2005–2006	4802.41
2004–2005	3848.29
2003–2004	3371.97
2002–2003	3061.97
2001–2002	2501.13
2000–2001	1882.10
1999–2000	1949.32
1998–1999	1705.74
1997–1998	1525.43
1996–1997	1475.42
1995–1996	1217.06
1994–1995	1197.63
1993–1994	1088.72
1992–1993	944.57
1991–1992	849.66
1990–1991	763.91

Source Bangladesh Bank (http://www.bangladesh-bank.org/)
*Data up to month of May of financial year 2008–2009

A recent economic analysis pointed out that if entry quotas were increased by an amount equal to 3% of developed countries' labor forces, there would be an increase in world welfare 156 billion US $ per year (Winters et al. 2002). Bangladesh has no existing or proposed GATS commitments on Mode 4 in health services.

A study observed that Bangladesh would be benefited substantially through increased export of service providers through TMNP (Raihan and Mahmood 2004). This study designed three scenarios and observed that an increase in export of professionals involved in services (e.g., doctors) would bring more benefit and the potential benefit from exporting about 0.2 million professionals would be around 11.57 billion US dollar (Raihan and Mahmood 2004). On the other hand exporting unskilled and semiskilled workers, the study observed had lower levels of return.

To examine the causes behind employing foreign doctors in the private hospitals (TMNP from foreign land), a survey was conducted on four large private hospitals with the help of checklists. It was observed that having good qualifications, good caring attitude toward patients, having well training and professional attitude and competency of the doctors were major reasons for employing foreign doctors in the country by the hospitals. Persons affiliated with the hospitals mentioned that problems associated with income tax and work permit issues, hiring right doctors

Table 3.21 Reasons for employing foreign doctors in the hospital (one dot represents one hospital)

Causes	Strongly disagree	Disagree	Undecided	Agree	Strongly agree
Have higher degrees/qualifications				●	●●●
Less costly than locals	●●●	●			
Well mannered				●	●●●
Very caring to patients					●●●●
Well trained					●●●●
They attract more local patients				●●	●●
Patients like them				●	●●●
Doctors add fame and name to hospital				●	●●●
Have professional attitude					●●●●
Doctors are more competent					●●●●

Source Field Survey (2009)

and restrictions from the government, etc., actually create barriers in employing doctors in the private hospitals of the country.

These above problems should be solved for the sake of smooth health service trading among the SAARC countries. Like the foreign doctors and nurses who are currently employed in the private hospitals in Bangladesh, Bangladeshi doctors can work in the SAARC countries. This will enhance human resource trading among SAARC countries (Tables 3.21 and 3.22).

Temporary Movement of Natural Person (TMNP): Opportunities and Barriers for Bangladesh

To address the interest of the developing countries and promote service trade, the ongoing round of GATS negotiations must aim at liberalizing movement of natural persons. Mode 4 liberalization could be a win-win situation for both developed and developing countries.

There are several barriers to health service trade through Mode 4 of GATS. Several restrictions are imposed on health service providers who intend to move to a host country. These can be broadly grouped into the following categories (Chanda 2001).

- Immigration-related regulations which block entry and stay of service providers;

Table 3.22 Problems faced in employing foreign doctors in the hospital (one dot represents one hospital)

Problems	Strongly disagree	Disagree	Undecided	Agree	Strongly agree
Cultural barrier/language barrier		●●		●●	
Problems in hiring right doctors			●	●●	●
Problems associated with government work permit issue			●	●●	●
Problems associated with income tax				●●●	●
Licensing problem		●●	●●		
Foreign exchange restrictions			●	●●	
Problems involved in document requirements by the government			•	●	●●
Restrictions on employing foreign doctors by the government				●●	●●
Restrictions from Bangladesh Medical and Dental Association (BMDC)			●●●	●	

Source Field Survey (2009)

- Regulations concerning recognition of qualifications, certification, licensing, work experience and training;
- Differential treatment of domestic and foreign service personnel.

A number of recent decisions have been made by the Government of Bangladesh with a new foreign doctor/nurse employment policy, which creates barrier for foreign doctors and nurses to work in the country (MOHFW, Advertisement, Date: 28/6/2009). The policy states that if there is any dearth of Bangladeshi specialist doctor within the country, only then a hospital can take initiative to employ foreign specialist doctors. Besides, a hospital must employ at least two Bangladeshi doctors, against the employment of one foreign specialist doctor, and the number of foreign doctors should not exceed more than one-fifth of the total number of recommended doctors working in a hospital (this rule will remain valid for first 7 years). There is also limit on visa for the foreign doctors and nurses. Although the whole procedure of getting employment is complex, foreign doctors and nurses can practice in the country after taking permission from the government and Bangladesh Medical and Dental Association (BMDC) with making formal applications (A-IV).

A large number of Bangladeshi doctors mostly non-specialist doctors are working in the Middle Eastern countries, and it seems that there exist good opportunities for Bangladeshi doctors to work abroad.[6] This is a significant positive sign for Bangladesh indeed. Bangladesh can adopt some domestic policies in this respect. For opening up market in the SAARC region and also in the developed countries, government should identify current capacity of supply of health professionals within the country. Bangladeshi nurses, though in a very limited number, are already serving with good reputation abroad. If some manpower-exporting firms take an interest in establishing training institutes for nurses of international standard, then the initiative can fetch handsome returns in the long run. Any type of investor in the private sector can set up such institutes with a vision for their prospects in the foreign employment markets. Government of Bangladesh may take the lead in providing training facilities for nurses with the objective of creating a surplus number to feed the needs of foreign countries.

Liberalization of Trade in Health Services in Bangladesh: Challenges and Opportunities

It is generally observed that service trade is considerably heavily restricted than goods trade. As international health service transactions include foreign direct investment (FDI) and the movement of labor, as well as long-established cross-border transactions, any policy that impedes service producers and consumers' act together through any of these channels (or modes of supply) is considered an hindrance to trade (Findlay and Warren 2000).

The major opportunities and risks for health service trade in developing countries like Bangladesh are mentioned in Table 36. Impediments to trade in health services come mostly in the form of non-tariff barriers (NTBs), reflecting the difficulties inherent in imposing tariffs directly upon either the service consumer or the service supplier as they interact across borders. NTBs are always difficult to measure. The lack of information on impediments to trade and investment in services, and the consequent impact on the economy of these impediments, reduces the set of tools that policy reformers can use when pushing for liberalization (Belsky et al. 2004) (Tables 3.23 and 3.24).

[6]Recently, the High Commissioner of Bhutan in Bangladesh has expressed his interest to employ Bangladeshi physicians in Bhutan. He conveyed the message of his government to employ Bangladeshi physicians in Bhutan in a meeting held in Dhaka. It may be mentioned here that a significant number of students from Bhutan are receiving medical education in Bangladesh (*Prothom Alo*, July 6, 2009).

Table 3.23 Four large private hospitals in Dhaka

Name of the hospitals	Investment and partners	Number of foreign doctors	Number of foreign nurses	Number of doctors	Number of nurses	Administration and employees
Square Hospitals, private hospital, Dhaka, Bangladesh 18-storied, 300-bed hospital	42 million US $; the square hospital is an affiliate partner of Methodist Healthcare, Memphis, Tennessee, USA; Christian Medical College, Vellore, India; and Care IVF (In Vitro Fertility Centre) Centre, Singapore	Total 25 (India, Pakistan, Singapore, Thailand, England)	Philippines, Australia, Sri Lanka and India (30)	350 (approximately)	300 (approximately)	Over 1000
United Hospitals	Management partnership with KPJ Healthcare Berhad of Malaysia	10	India (30)	120	75	150
Apollo Hospital Dhaka 450-bed super -specialty hospital built in a total area of 400,000 sq. ft.	45 million US $, STS Holdings Ltd. the promoter of Apollo Hospital	India (20)	India and Sri Lanka (45)	Not known	550	1400
Z H Sikder Cardiac Care and Research Centre	100% Own	10	–	–	–	–

Source http://www.skyscrapercity.com/showthread.php?t=196333&page=4; New Age (2006), News Today (2005); Field Survey (2009)

Table 3.24 Brief outline of trade in health services in Bangladesh

Macroeconomic and trade environment • Bangladesh is a least developed country (LDC) with GDP per capita US $ 1500 (2008) • Liberal market access and national treatment policies allowing up to 100% foreign equity participation in most sectors and does not require a economic needs test	*State of the domestic healthcare system* • Health status indicators: population growth rate 1.292%; birth rate: 28.86 births/1000 population; death rate: 8 deaths/1000 population; infant mortality rate: 59.02/100 live births; total fertility rate: 2.74%
Mode 1: Cross-border supply of health services • Telemedicine services across borders are currently practiced by some hospitals and private organizations • No restrictions exist on services and products available on the Internet for personal use • There does not exist any government policy on telemedicine services. As a result, no controls/obstacles to use this service • IT infrastructure is good; the rate of Internet subscribers is around 7.3 persons/1000 population • Bangladesh has no existing GATS commitments in Mode 1 in health services	*Mode 2: Consumption of health services abroad* • Bangladesh is a net importer of health service. Countries receiving Bangladeshi patients are mainly from India, Thailand, Singapore and Malaysia • No restrictions on private citizens going abroad for consumption of health services • No existing or proposed GATS commitments in any health-related sub-sectors under Mode 2
Mode 3: Foreign commercial presence • Commercial presence requires that foreign service providers incorporate or establish the business locally in accordance with the relevant provisions of Bangladesh laws, rules and regulations. There is no fixed ratio of equity between local and foreign investors. Foreign equity to the extent of 100% is allowed • Difficult to identify FDI in health sector as all private hospitals • Ministry of commerce and industry is responsible for regulating FDI in health. Licensing of premises and its compliance with standards is the responsibility of MOH • Bangladesh has no existing or proposed GATS commitments on Mode 3 in health services	*Mode 4: Movement of health professionals* • In Bangladesh, the entry and residence of foreign natural persons (service providers) are subjected to Bangladesh's immigration and labor laws, regulations, guidelines and procedures. There is no restriction issuing work permits to foreign nationals in Bangladesh. The employment of foreign natural persons for the implementation of the foreign investment shall be agreed upon by the contracting parties and approved by the government, and such personnel shall be employed in higher management and specialized jobs only • There is no restriction on professionals to move abroad for temporary job • Bangladesh has no existing or proposed GATS commitments on Mode 4 in health services

While addressing the issue related to GATS and its influence on health policy of Bangladesh, it is observed that GATS may have some adverse affect on the health service policy of the country. The GATS actually works in the following manner: GATS commits WTO members to successive rounds of negotiations with a view to achieving a progressively higher level of liberalization in their service sectors. To achieve this, WTO members make liberalization requests of other member countries in secret, bilateral meetings in Geneva so as to open up to competition those sectors which are of most interest to their own service providers (Khor 2006).

When a country fully commits a given sector, e.g., health service sector under the GATS, it accepts two types of legal obligations. It actually grants 'market access' to foreign competitors and refrains itself from establishing barriers to trade, such as quotas that limit the number of providers of a given service (physicians, hospitals, etc.). It also abstains from establishing barriers to the volume of service supplied by each provider (e.g., number of bed). If Bangladesh commits fully, it agrees to treat foreign competitors no less favorably than the suppliers from its own country (Belsky et al. 2004).

Although developing countries officially have the right to decide whether to commit a sector to GATS, in practice they come under intense pressure in these negotiations to meet the demands of more powerful WTO members—pressure which the smaller and poorer countries are often powerless to resist.

From a health policy perspective, measures that restrict market access may be more important than measures that restrict national treatment (Blouin 2006). Restricting market access may serve legitimate health policy objectives, such as limitations on the number of service suppliers in a geographical area based on an economic needs test (Blouin 2006). If Bangladesh would like to open its health sector to foreign providers, it should consider 'experimenting with liberalization outside of GATS before making GATS commitments as policy reversal remains easier if the experiment produces unsatisfactory results (Khor 2006).

Liberalization of trade in health services can create opportunities for Bangladesh, but may also aggravate preexisting problems. Moreover, once liberalization is locked in under international trade agreements, reversing policies becomes difficult. This may be true for a poor country like Bangladesh. It is understood that making inappropriate commitments to liberalize health services under GATS may result in the loss of policy space for Bangladesh.

The barriers to trade in services are opaque, given the nature of transactions involved. Trade in health services, far more than trade in goods, is affected by a variety of domestic regulations, ranging from qualification and licensing requirements and procedures in professional services regulations in telecommunications, and other network services, to universal access requirements in health services (Mattoo and Sauvé 2003). There are several barriers between India and Bangladesh which are responsible for rise in informal trade in health services between the two countries (Table 3.25).

Conclusion

The South Asian Association for Regional Cooperation (SAARC) was established when its charter was formally adopted on December 8, 1985, by the heads of state or Government of Bangladesh, Bhutan, India, Maldives, Nepal, Pakistan and Sri

Table 3.25 Opportunities and risk of liberalizing international trade in health services in developing countries

Mode of supply	Importing country		Exporting country	
	opportunities	Risks	Opportunities	Risks
Cross-border supply	• Improved access to high-quality diagnostic and therapeutic services • Service extendable to remote and underserved areas • Upgraded skills, dissemination of knowledge through interactive electronic means	• Capital intensive, possible diversion of resources from basic preventive and curative services • May hurt equity if it caters to only the affluent segment of the population • Difficulties in regulating e-prescriptions	• Increased revenue generation	• Problems of electronic transfer of revenue from developing countries
Consumption abroad	• Overcome shortages of physical and human resources in specialized fields • Contractual arrangement with exporting country to rationalize costs	• High foreign exchange consumption by poor governments • Mainly the well to do benefit	• Promote 'medical tourism' • Increased revenue generation	• 'Crowding out' of nationals, especially the less well to do • Create dual market structure

(continued)

Table 3.25 (continued)

Mode of supply	Importing country		Exporting country	
	opportunities	Risks	Opportunities	Risks
Foreign commercial presence	• Foreign direct investment in health infrastructure • Employment opportunities for local workforce • Possible freeing up of local resources • Access to higher-quality health services	• 'Internal' brain drain of health professionals • Establishment of a two-tiered system: 'crowding out' of poor, 'skimming' of lucrative patients • Challenge of regulating foreign investors • If subsidies used, potential diversion of resources from the public sector	• Increased revenue generation	• Similar to an investor in any other sector
Movement of natural persons	• In the short run, achieves a balanced health workforce, which could be deployed in remote areas	• In the long run, mitigates against nationalization of health workforce	• Upgraded skills of providers on return to home country • Workforce in labor surplus countries to cater for others • Increased revenue generation	• External brain drain of skilled workforce • Loss of investment in financial capital and subsidized training • Temporary migration of workforce may result in permanent loss

Source World Health Organization (WHO)

Lanka. Countries belonging to South Asian region have already liberalized their service sectors to a certain extent through unilateral, multilateral and regional initiatives. Under the GATS, most South Asian countries (other than Bhutan) have made commitments. Further commitments are forthcoming under regional and bilateral arrangements such as Bay of Bengal Initiative for Multi-Sectoral Technical and Economic Cooperation (BIMSTEC)—including Bangladesh, India, Bhutan, Nepal and Sri Lanka—and the Comprehensive Economic Partnership Agreement (CEPA) between India and Sri Lanka (Kelegama 2009).

Trade in services is also expected to find its way into the South Asian Free Trade Area (SAFTA) framework (Kalegama 2009). The idea seems to broaden SAFTA so that liberalization in goods gets a stimulus from services. There also seems to be an observation that the services in South Asia have more complementarities than the trade in goods. The SAARC Summit of the Heads of States (Dhaka, 12–13, November 2005) recognized the potential for trade in services which has rapidly expanded at the informal level. At the 14th Summit (New Delhi, April 3–4, 2007), the leaders stressed that to realize the full potential, SAFTA should integrate trade in services.

Bangladesh also joined the Bay of Bengal Initiative for Multi-Sectoral Technical and Economic Cooperation (BIMSTEC). There is another regional agreement in the process of forming an FTA that would include Nepal, Bhutan, Thailand, Myanmar and India. Bangladesh is discussing bilateral free trade agreements (FTAs) with India, Pakistan and Sri Lanka. It has recently finalized a Trade and Investment Framework Agreement (TIFA) with the USA (Bhattacharya 2005). In the context of the present multilateral trading system, every country is trying to transform the challenges of globalization into opportunities for economic prosperity.

SAFTA will provide a mechanism for enhancing intra-SAARC trade, and Bangladesh can reap the benefit of regional cooperation. Both India and Bangladesh have long shared common objectives for closer economic integration within the South Asian region. These have recently been reemphasized by signing on to SAFTA4, which takes effect from January 2006.

Some initiatives have been taken under SAFTA in this respect. These include the eventual removal of tariffs and non-tariff barriers on trade between the members, the harmonization of custom procedures and documentation, the facilitation of banking relationships, and cooperation and improvements in the infrastructure for regional trade (World Bank 2006). All these may have favorable effect on health service trade among SAARC countries.

A number of studies have observed that there is a high potential of gains from Mode 4. The gain is huge in terms of financial aspect. Winters et al. (2002) indicate that large potential gains may come from a small increase in the movement of people between low- and high-income countries. They suggest that increasing developed country quota for incoming temporary movement of natural persons by three percent of the existing labor will generate global income gains of US $510 billion per year (Winters et al. 2002). A modest liberalization of this scale may provide large benefits for the developed countries.

To achieve success in regional health service trade, countries under SAARC region should take positive steps such as remove visa requirements, remove limitations on the movement of natural persons, establish common curricula in medical education, mutual recognition of diploma and other professional qualifications, and ease requirements of obtaining necessary permits and authorizations. These policies, if implemented, would enhance health service trade substantially among the countries under the SAARC region.

Chapter 4
Health Sector Scenarios in Sri Lanka: Policy Designing and Implications

Sahana Roy Chowdhury

Introduction

In the year 2005, WHO adopted the resolution that all countries across the globe should start extending and facilitating access to all essential health services to all its citizens so that catastrophic health shocks are completely eliminated from the economies. While the MDGs emphasised on piecemeal steps towards achieving small target indicators such as MMR and IMR, SDGs take a holistic approach; therefore, targets before the countries have become more stringent. From governance point of view, the most critical step lies in defining "all essential health services", which WHO has enlisted, which is suggestive in nature since regions and countries do vary in terms of the type, severity and extent of diseases that they are exposed to, and the kind of health concerns that they already have. The landmark report of WHO released in 2010 [*Health systems financing—the path to universal coverage*] mentions that health financing is a major concern and a big hindrance in achieving UHC, especially in the low-income countries. The report mentions that on an average, at least 4–5% of GDP is required to reach the UHC goal. The out-of-pocket expenditure as a proportion of total expenditure has also been taken as an important indicator of vulnerability; if the health expenditure falls below 15–20% of the total expenditure, it might have catastrophic wealth shocks implication for low-income economies, it states. Based on GDP growth targets, the Lancet Commission 2013 had projected that a 3% health expenditure in low-income countries (LICs) would significantly improve the health indicators by 2035. It depends upon innovative ways to design and identify the financing mechanisms, efficiency of revenue collection and prioritisation of the governing bodies to channelise resources towards the health sector. Plentiful evidences are there on more health expenditures leading to better health outcomes. On the other hand, evidences on wasteful expenditures: more in revenue form and

---

S. Roy Chowdhury (✉)
International Management Institute, Kolkata, India
e-mail: s.roychowdhury@imi-k.edu.in

A. Banik (ed.), *Trade in Health Services in South Asia*,
https://doi.org/10.1007/978-981-15-2191-1_4

insignificant in capital form, leading to less than expected health outcomes in the medium to longer run is also not scarce. Therefore, quality spending has also been emphasised as a new dimension while emphasising on achieving the UHC targets.

Trends in Global Health Spending Towards UHC

The WHO special reports and policy papers show that global health expenditure is rapidly increasing, faster than the gross domestic product of countries and the growth is higher in low- and middle-income countries (6% on average as compared to 4% in high income countries). Globally, OOP expenditure has gone down[1] and pooled funds from governments' sources have increased quite a bit. If we look into the type of global health spending, low- and medium-income countries spend more than 50% of their health spending on primary health care (PHC), however, public spending is less than 40% of total PHC spending. Surprisingly, immunisation spending still remains to be heavily dependent on external funding for many low-income countries. Over time, many low- and middle-income countries have taken health expenditure as priorities and have increased expenditure to a remarkable extent. If we make an intra-regional comparison, Sri Lanka's current health expenditure, among its peer low–middle-income countries, is remarkably high and increasing overtime (Fig. 4.1c). The global health expenditure database 2016 published by WHO shows that the world spent 10% of GDP in health, average per capita was $1000 but 50% of the world spent less than $350 per person (Fig. 4.2). This implies that inequality in global spending has increased to a very large extent. Countries define primary healthcare services in different ways; therefore, categorisation of data for comparison purpose is difficult and one of the biggest hurdles in creating large or global health database. Public spending in all type of countries has increased in per capita terms. However, health spending as a share has not increased to a noticeable extent in LICs (Fig. 4.3).

As it has been already defined that UHC refers to the access to health by all people without having financial hardship, this involves strengthening of health financing and governance to deliver quality health services at reasonably low cost. The progress towards UHC is typically measured by two indicators: service coverage and financial protection. The WB and WHO find the determinants of UHC service coverage and not surprisingly, they have shown that countries having higher per capita income have done better on that front than others (Fig. 4.4); however, it depends upon country's priorities as well—Kenya and Vietnam did much well in spite of having low per capita GDP. On the front of catastrophic health spending (CHS), the literature suggests that it is not necessarily true that as UHC coverage increases CHS falls (Fig. 4.5), which implies that policymakers in different countries do provide wider service coverage but may not include priority items, or necessary items may not be offered at cheaper cost. Policy implication may be that service coverage should be done on the basis of people covered but also on the basis of share of expenditure that people make in the

[1]Refer Fig. 4.1.

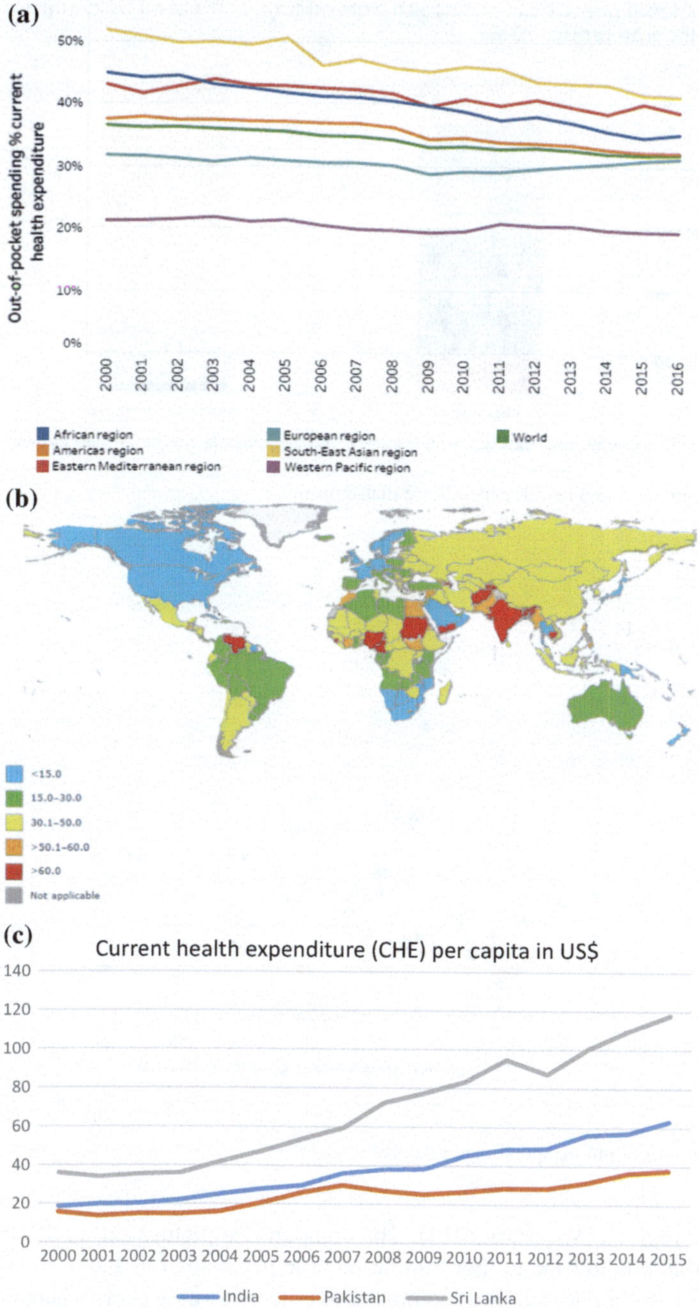

Fig. 4.1 Health expenditure pattern across the globe. **a** Out-of-pocket expenditure as % of total expenditure. **b** Out-of-pocket expenditure as % of total expenditure—world map. **c** Intra-regional comparison of health expenditure

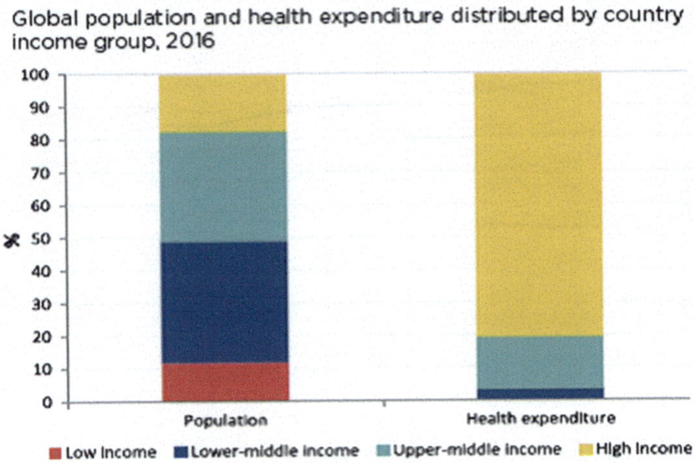

Fig. 4.2 Population and health expenditure distribution

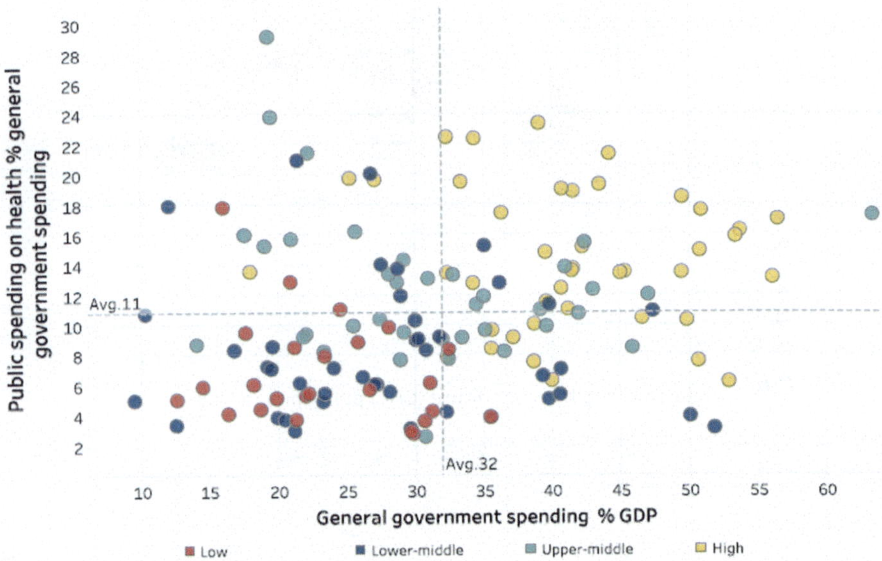

Fig. 4.3 Pattern of public spending on health

respective regions (Wagstaff 2014). The comparative picture shows that Sri Lanka is doing much better than other middle-income peers such as India; the CHS does not increase, rather decreases as compared to other emerging peers where population pressure poverty has been major contributing factors behind increasing CHS.

Fig. 4.4 Universal health coverage index: A global comparison

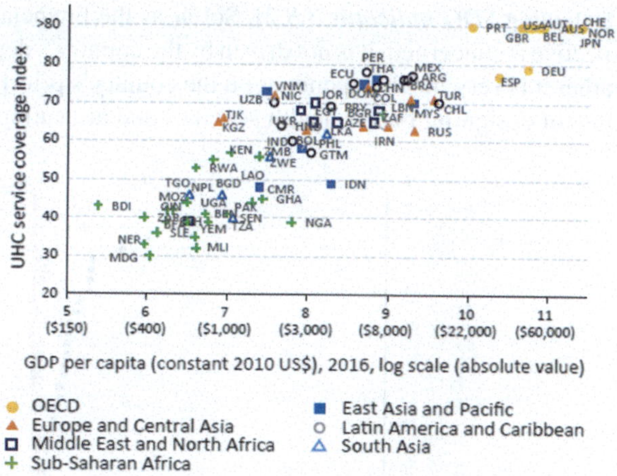

Fig. 4.5 Catastrophic health spending: A global comparison

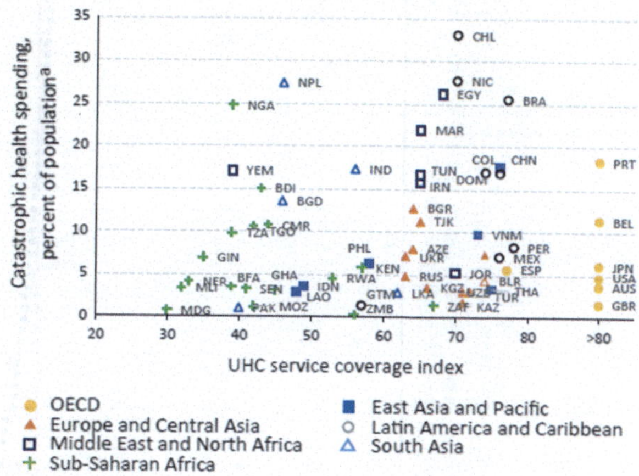

Global monitoring report 2017 brought out by WHO shows that at least 50% of population cannot obtain essential health services and for almost 100 million people find it high enough to push them into extreme poverty: less than $1.90 per day. Notably, access to essential health services varies across countries although government expenditure remains similar, implying simple increase in public expenditure may not have been equally effective across countries. Second big observation that the WHO report emphasises is that the service coverage has increased more due to income rise rather than public spending rise. The UHC service coverage index consisting of 11 tracer indicators mostly includes primary healthcare. The relation between public share in total health spending and performance towards UHC service delivery is ambiguous, and more research is needed to be done to understand the driving forces. Another major finding is that the countries that have had larger public share in health spending tended to have lower incidence of catastrophic health spending, defined by people spending more than 10% of their household budget in health [following *SDG indicator 3.8.2*]. So far as the financial protection from equity perspective is concerned, it is not driven by the country's dependence on public spending; rather it is very much dependant on the country's priorities on equity concerns at the time of designing public health schemes and allocating public spending (Fig. 4.6).

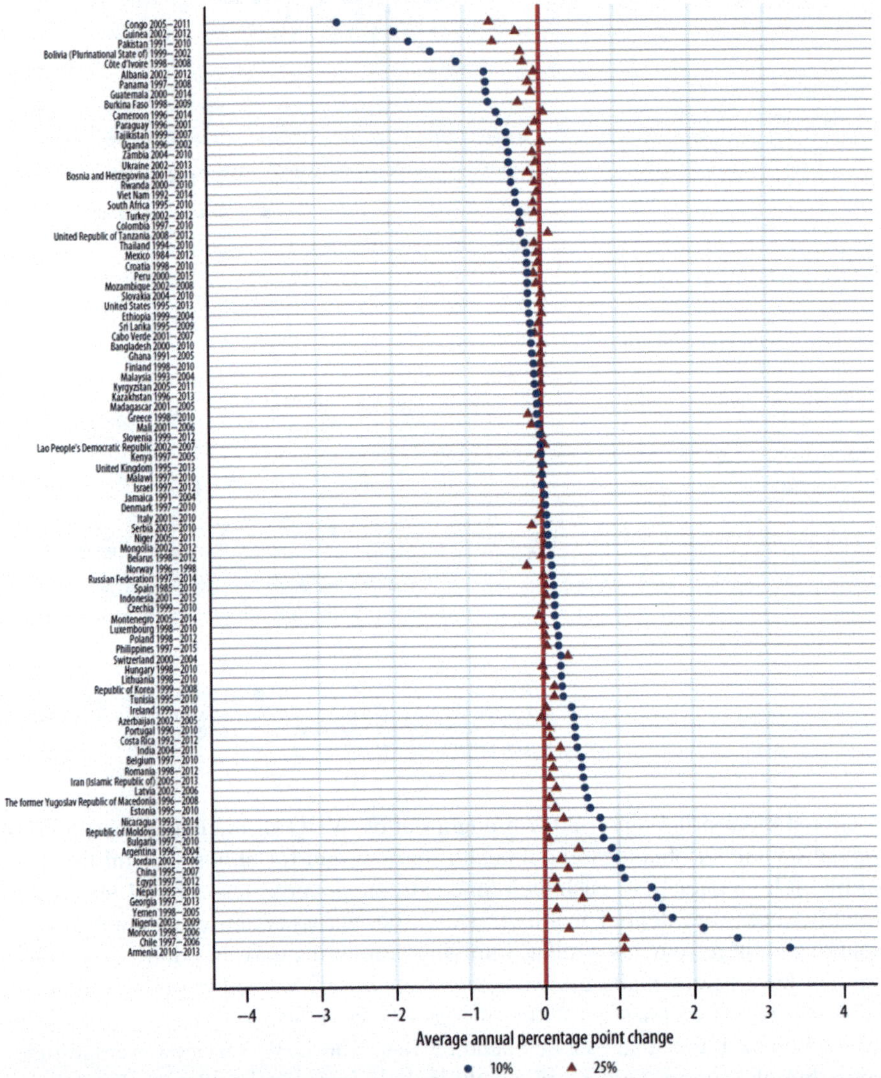

Notes: WHO and World Bank estimated values are based on standard definitions and methods to ensure cross-country comparability which may not correspond to the methods used at regional and/or national level to monitor catastrophic spending on health. Global estimates are based on data available for global monitoring which may not necessarily align with availability of data at national or regional levels.

Source: Global database on financial protection assembled by WHO and the World Bank.

Fig. 4.6 Catastrophic health scenario: A global comparison

The Health Scenario of Sri Lanka: Big Challenges

It is predicted that by 2030 one in every 5 people will be aged 60 or above making Sri Lanka South Asia's most rapidly ageing country. Policymakers have also perceived the fact that an ageing country should continuously increase investment to make people's live longer. Sri Lanka has shown a track record of simultaneously achieving an efficient pro-poor health coverage at low cost. This has not been observed in similar low–middle-income countries in the last 50 years. However, as it has been identified by many researchers, the cornerstone of UHC in Sri Lanka is that it has been completely supply side: unlike in many countries where targeting and identifying poor are sought for. Also, there is limited performance linked or output-based financing of healthcare providers, no conditional cash transfer or social health insurance, which are desirable dimensions towards achieving UHC (Smith 2018, WB-UHC study series no. 38). Sri Lanka's government health spending as share of GDP is low by regional standard, and out-of-pocket expenditure (OOP) is also around 40% (Fig. 4.1b). On the financial efficiency front, a common claim that the report emphasises on is that high budget or higher share to primary care need not necessarily lead to better outcomes in case of Sri Lanka. Emphasis should be more on better governance better incentive designing of health schemes to get effective outcomes.

On the performance scale, Sri Lanka has been one of the best performers among its South Asian peers. It started targeting MDGs in the 1990s and could achieve them in 2015. It has successfully eliminated the communicable diseases, such as malaria, polio, measles, tetanus, or could bring its outcomes closer to the near elimination levels. Health financing indicators have also been favourable: government expense has generally been 1.5% of GDP. Big challenge and a difference in approach have been observed with regard to its supply-side intervention, whereas mist of the low–middle-income countries have emphasised on demand-side intervention by proper identification of poor (Cotlear and Smith 2015).

Sri Lanka's health system is financed by the Ministry of Health and its nine provincial counterparts from general tax revenues, but it coexists with large private sector which is funded though OOP expenses and are highly staffed quite often, with off-duty government health personnel. So far as the geographical access indicator is concerned, Sri Lanka has performed well; on an average, households are only 2.5 kms away from maternity clinics and almost 93% of population is within 15 kms from a hospital. The government procures pharmaceuticals directly but not in sufficient qualities due to budget constraint; this needs serious policy focus. Nonetheless, on the one hand, strong quality service delivery of Sri Lanka's supply-driven health system has taken a large step towards meeting UHC while, on the other hand, the quality service provided at a cheap cost has widened the demand–supply gap further, which has posed a governance challenge. Most interestingly, residency is the basis of getting all kinds of medical facilities. In fact, non-residents such as migrants do typically get free medical care. Thus, on coverage ground, it is ahead of many advanced countries with regard to UHC. However, as mentioned, the scope of the medical facilities provided are not demand based, rather budget determined, which

Table 4.1 UHC coverage indicators tracer

	Sri Lanka (%)	Lower-middle income (%)
Prevention and health promotion		
Family planning	68	46
Antenatal care	99	86
Skilled birth attendance	99	74
DPT3 immunisation	99	86
Tobacco nonus	85	78
Access to improved water	94	83
Access to improved sanitation	92	59
Treatment		
Antiretroviral therapy	19	29
Tuberculosis	86	82
Hypertension	21	27
Diabetes	10	11

Source World development indicators

poses a problem in Sri Lanka where medical facilities are provided at cheaper cost but are of good quality, and therefore has an ever-increasing demand for it. As it is found from Table 1 where the data source is World Bank's World Development Indicators (WDI), that so far as antenatal health care, immunisation coverage are concerned, Sri Lanka has attended 100% mark but when it comes to non-communicable diseases, the indicators are not at all satisfactory. While analysing whether OOP expenditure is catastrophic in nature, it was found that this expenditure has not turned out to be impoverishing. Intra-regional comparison also shows that Sri Lanka has a wider UHC coverage as compared to its South Asian emerging peers in terms of the UHC coverage index of WHO 2017 (Fig. 4.7).

Externalities in the Healthcare Systems Design: Role of Private Sector

At present, 50% of the health expenditure relates to the private sector in Sri Lanka. When health schemes are rolled out to enhance the coverage retaining much of the purchases and provisioning with the private sector, there are visible differences in countries' concomitant rise in health expenditures; Maldives opened up such UHC to cover citizens with a dollar limit (US$6500) in 2012 and it was done through

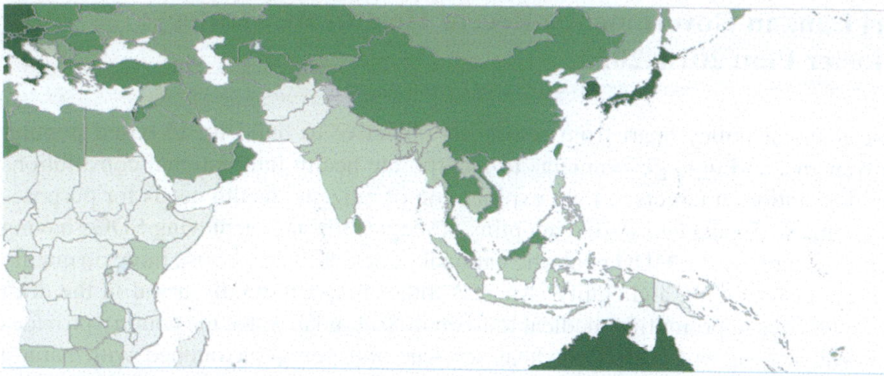

Fig. 4.7 UHC coverage index. *Source* WHO UHC data portal, WHO 2017

PPP: government and a private insurance company; it was found that national health expenditure increased to 11.5% of GDP in 2015 from 8.1% of GDP in 2008. On the other hand, Thailand started similar coverage scheme in 2001 retaining purchase and much of the provision under public sector it could manage to universalise access to the country's urban and rural poor at expenditure less than 4% of GDP. Consequent upon SDG 3.8.2 on universalisation of health coverage, WHO's emphasis on designing UHC target indicators underscores population coverage and service comprehensiveness, but rarely gauge private sector's participation and its consequences on the country's health system; especially when this relates to low–middle-income countries. While judging UHC, it should also be taken into account that whether it is truly universal and equitable rather than looking into the population coverage numbers and not the economic ramifications of increasing private participation.

Sri Lanka had emphasised on primary health care from the very beginning of designing strategies towards healthcare policies and systems. This has helped them to fast-track and streamline their healthcare services network towards international targets set in recent decades, which emphasises more on preventive and primary health care rather than curative healthcare, secondary and tertiary healthcare services. Another very important dimension which is often overlooked while framing policies towards UHC is the linkage between education and health achievements; especially the average education level of female household members and the health outcomes. Sri Lanka performed remarkably well post-independence because of its high female literacy at the household level. Also, universalisation of education simultaneously, as a policy measure has created huge externality and pushed further the health management systems towards success. In addition, some strategic steps such as providing permission to the health personnel to work in private sector after duty hours have enabled creating low cost but widely available health service providers, which remains a big challenge in many of the low–middle-income countries still now.

Sri Lankan Government's Recent Healthcare Strategy: Master Plan 2016–2025

The national policy apart from setting its objective to build broad-based popular movements and urge governments to incorporate health into national constitutions and legislation, it targets to fight exploitation of citizens' health needs for purposes of profit. Sri Lanka had started adopting strategies towards achieving SDGs having achieved already the MDG goals the national policy draft emphasise more on quality service provisioning and equity issues. Another major issue discussed in the draft policy relates to promoting medical tourism in Sri Lanka. Since the country provides relatively cheap but quality medical services and being surrounded with natural resources, have made Sri Lanka a travel destination for many neighbouring countries. If this opportunity is suitably utilised, Sri Lanka can build an efficient network of medical service infrastructure and network with the help of the foreign currency they earn in the tourism sector. Therefore, the national policy underscores the importance of building a strong synergy between their tourism sector and the health sector in order to reap the maximum benefit out of these burgeoning sectors.

Sri Lanka's Health Financing Pattern and Challenges

Sri Lanka, as already it has been described, could successfully hit the MDG targets in providing quality healthcare services at cheap cost. However, given the changing demographic and increasing private sector share in healthcare financing have posed serious challenges to the sustenance of Sri Lanka's health financing policy. As the literature depicts, there are four basic healthcare financing models across the globe. The Beveridge model—healthcare is provided and financed by the government (Britain, Spain, Scandinavian and New Zealand); Bismarck model—uses an insurance model where insurance is paid by the employees and employers through a payroll deduction (Germany, France, Japan, Belgium and Switzerland), national health insurance model—it is a mix of the earlier two models which uses private providers but paid by government run insurance companies. Therefore, the last one is the OOP model, which is mostly used by the poor countries. Here, cost sharing, self-medication and other expenditures are done solely by private households (Madurawela 2016). Sri Lanka's government health expenditure was 3.5% of GDP in 2014 with 56% public funding and 44% private funding. Most of the government funding is done by Ministry of Health (MoH) and rest by Provincial Department of Health (DOH). Estimation shows that Sri Lanka's 60+ population will double between 2011 and 2041 and will be 5.4 million nearly. Further, the share of this category of population will be 24.8 from 12.5 in 2011. Therefore, elderly care as a different dimension of healthcare services should be emphasised as a new policy initiative. This includes more chronic diseases, such as lung, liver diseases, diabetes, cardio-vascular diseases, treatments to which are relatively costly. Also, it has been stated by many researchers that Sri Lanka is having an epidemiological transition implying change in the pattern of mortality and disease from communicable to non-communicable type. Government hospital data also show that NDCs-related deaths are on rise and this type of disease burden imposes more economic strain than communicable diseases. Inadequate resource mobilisation has been detected to be a big reason behind Sri Lanka's perceived vulnerable health financing situation in near future. Researchers also raise questions in Sri Lanka's health financing over its allocative efficiency: Patients typically bypass primary health care (PHC) and spend a lot on secondary or tertiary (STHC) health care which is quite evident in almost 65–70% contribution of STHC in total recurrent healthcare expenditure.

There are some suggestive indicators given by WHO for the Asia-Pacific region, which need to be monitored while designing a country's health financing strategies. It says that the OOP should not exceed 30–40% of total health expenditure (THE) and THE should be at least 4–5% of GDP; over 90% of the population should be covered under pre-payment and risk-pooling schemes and 100% of the vulnerable population should be covered under social assistance and safety-net programs.[2] Looking at Sri Lanka's indicators and comparing with what have been suggested, it seems that Sri Lanka is yet to explore different innovative mechanisms on health financing reform in order to broaden the coverage, scope of healthcare services delivered but at the same time, keeping an eye on the cost dimension. Due to large informal sector in Sri Lanka, it is not feasible to incorporate all the citizens under an umbrella Social Health Insurance Scheme where collection of contribution, registration, contracting and reimbursement will be a daunting administrative task for Sri Lanka. User-fee as a revenue mobilisation mechanism has many good sides. Sri Lanka had introduced this long back which was later-on abolished but re-introduced in 1971. This is basically a small proportion of charge in OPD visits collected by the government which is then re-invested in the health sector again. This has two positive effects: a source of revenue and curb unnecessary STHC expenditure which is increasing in Sri Lanka at an alarming rate.

Mitigating Regional Disparity in Healthcare Financing and Health-Infrastructure Provisioning

In most of the less developed economies, the concentration of quality healthcare services and infrastructure facilities are concentrated in the urban areas and there is a huge rural–urban divide on this. Sri Lanka is not an exception where this rural–urban split is well recognised by the government and necessary policy measures have been designed. One of the solutions often suggested is telemedicine which is defined as usage of information and communication technology between sites to transfer medical information. In Sri Lanka, 85% of the population live in rural areas. Pavlovskaya (2013) and many others reported that telemedicine has made working

[2]WHO 2009: Health financial strategy for the Asia-Pacific region 2000–2015, Geneva.

of the health and community workers easier and more effective. Many advanced countries have extended help in the form of FDI or technology transfer agreements to facilitate this, for example, Japanese experts have shared knowledge and expertise such as high quality images, and interactive voice messages, etc., in the area of oral cancer in Sri Lanka. Earlier, they used to travel during emergencies, now with the advent of telemedicine, time and cost savings have become possible. But lack of awareness and acceptance by the villagers has become a hindrance between success and designs of such policy moves, as has been the case with many other similar countries (e.g., India). This can also mitigate the problem of shortage of staffs in interior rural areas where it is difficult to design proper incentive in order to induce public health staffs to render critical services.

Conclusion and Policy Implications

Sri Lanka has been recognised as one of the best performers in the health sector in the South Asian region. It has started designing effective policies long back in the pre-independence era, which has resulted in good outcomes in terms of most of the health indicators. Sri Lanka for its efficient health policies could achieve the MDGs set by the UN much ahead of its target time and has performed well in the domain of communicable diseases as compared to many of its low–middle-income peers in the same region. However, as described in the paper, certain subsectors need serious attention and improvement. Sri Lanka is undergoing rapid epidemiological transition with more observed NCD cases rather than communicable diseases, also old age population is on the rise, implying change in the pattern of disease dependency in the near future. Therefore, health policy preparedness is needed to accommodate this demographic transition. Sri Lanka has been quite well known for its cheap health services in the South Asian region, however, concerns over quality health service and equity in such services has been the focal points of policy discussions. On the designing of health schemes to meet the recently set SDG goals, such as UHC, Sri Lanka could plan for the UHC component of widening service delivery suitably, given its wide health coverage that was already prevailing in the public health system, but towards the health financing and catastrophic health need component Sri Lanka is yet to design credible and effective policy to meet the set targets under SDG. Lastly, and importantly, the healthcare dependency of the patients in the secondary and tertiary healthcare rather than the primary health care has been an outcome of an intrinsically erroneous healthcare system designing in Sri Lanka's public healthcare management. This needs to be addressed urgently.

References

Cotlear D, Smith O (2015) How 24 developing countries are implementing universal health coverage reforms from the bottom up. International Bank for Reconstruction and Development, The World Bank, Going Universal, 99455

Madurawela S (2016) Health care financing in Sri Lanka: challenges and alternatives. Srilanka state of the economy report, Chap 8

Pavlovskaya O (2013) E-healthcare system coming to Kazakhstan (technical report). United States Central Command, Tampa, FL

Wagstaff A (2014) Who benefits from government health spending and why? World Bank Policy research working paper no. 7044. Washington DC.

Chapter 5
Health Sector Scenarios in Pakistan: Policy Priorities and Challenges Ahead

Gaurav Kumar Jha and Sahana Roy Chowdhury

Introduction

The need for an affordable and accessible and equitable health care of a given quality is one of the key ingredients for inclusive development for any country. The disease burden is unpredictable and uncertain and can also impact the vulnerable and the poor at the margin very catastrophically. Despite the challenges faced by the government in providing accessible health care to the people, there have been commendable achievements in the health sector in Pakistan.

Over a 17-year period, while the total life expectancy at birth has increased steadily, the infant mortality rate (per 1000 live births) has steadily decreased (Fig. 5.1). Further, during the same period, Pakistan's crude death rates and total fertility rates have steadily declined (Fig. 5.2).

Infant mortality rate (per 1000 live births) or IMR is one of the most important indicators showing how a country is prioritizing on neonatal care in the healthcare sector and nutritional requirements thereafter, for infants' survival. Figure 5.4 reveals that the infant mortality rates (per 1000 live births) have consistently decreased in Pakistan and in South Asian countries over the 1990–2017 period. However, the average annual decrease in Pakistan is significantly less as compared to many other South Asian countries and even to the global average.

During this period, while the IMR for South Asia has annually decreased by an overall average of 3.3% and that of globally by 2.9%, the average annual decrease for Pakistan is only 2%. China on the other hand (Fig. 5.6) has shown the largest annual decrease in its IMR followed by Bangladesh, Bhutan, Nepal and India. Pakistan therefore needs to scale up its efforts immensely in decreasing the IMR and catch up with its counterparts.

G. K. Jha (✉)
Ministry of Finance, New Delhi, India

S. Roy Chowdhury
International Management Institute, Kolkata, India

A. Banik (ed.), *Trade in Health Services in South Asia*,
https://doi.org/10.1007/978-981-15-2191-1_5

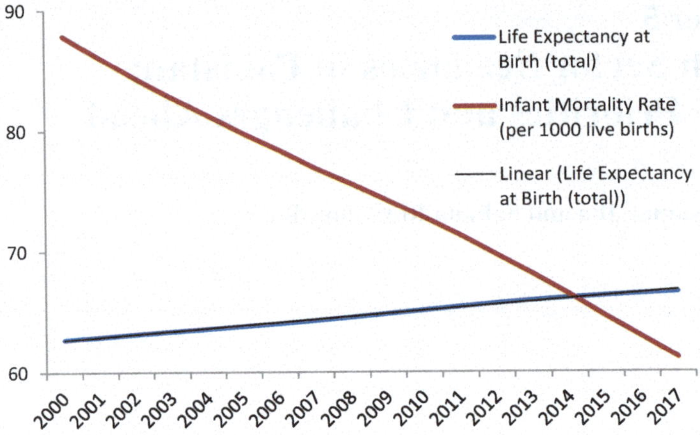

Fig. 5.1 Life expectancy at birth (total) and infant mortality rate (per 1000 live births), Pakistan

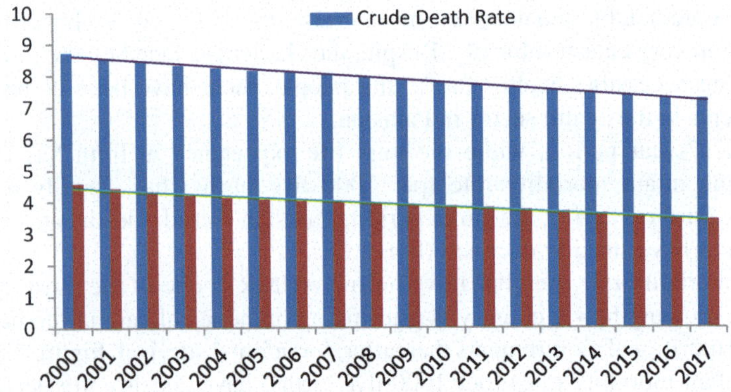

Fig. 5.2 Crude death rate and total fertility rate, Pakistan

Basic Health Indicators in Pakistan: An Analysis

An overview of the Pakistan's demographic and health indicators throws light on the overall health status of various segments of the population. The select indicators such as crude birth rate, crude death rate and total fertility rates have been declining. However, in comparison with the emerging economies, Pakistan needs to review its health policies to reduce under 5 mortality, neonatal mortality and maternal mortality rates. Even as compared to the rest of the world, Pakistan is lagging behind in each of these indicators (Fig. 5.3).

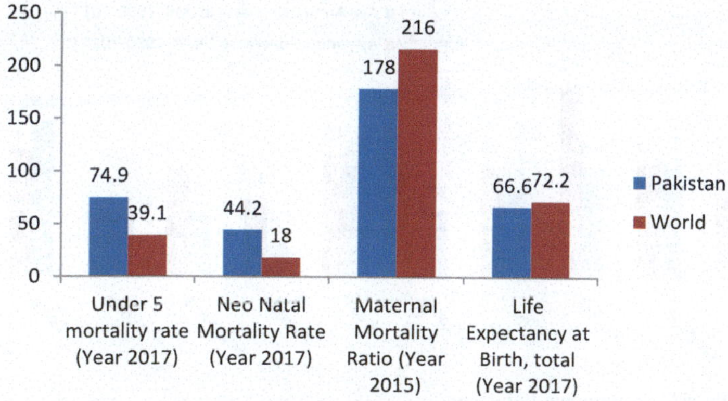

Source: World Development Indicators

Fig. 5.3 Comparison of select health indicators: Pakistan and World

Fig. 5.4 Comparison of infant mortality rates, per 1000 live births: Pakistan and South Asian Countries and World

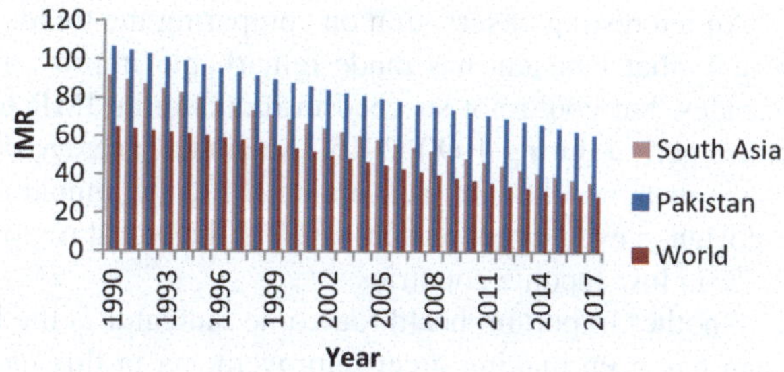

Source: World Development Indicators

Fig. 5.5 Comparison of maternal mortality ratio, per 100,000 live births: Pakistan and South Asian Countries and World

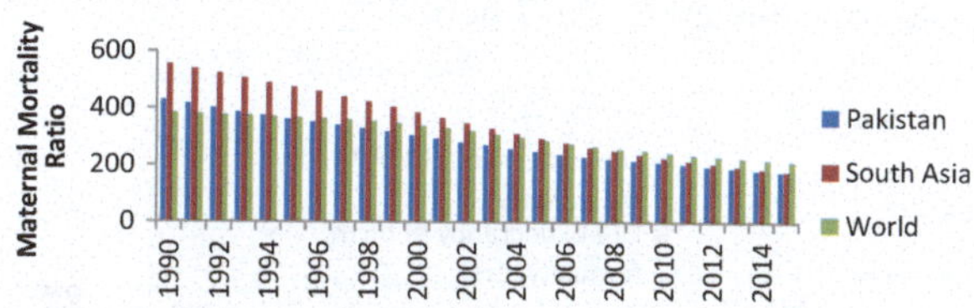

Source: World Development Indicators

Maternal mortality ratio (MMR) is another very important indicator to judge a country's health sector outcome and understand its policy priorities towards maternal health. This is measured per 100,000 live births. Figure 5.5 reveals that the maternal mortality rates (per 100,000 live births) have consistently decreased in Pakistan and in South Asian countries over the 1990–2015 period. If we compare this outcome with other low–middle-income peers in the same region, we find that the percentage average annual decrease in MMR is highest for Bhutan (7.1%) followed by China (5%) and then by Nepal (4.9%).

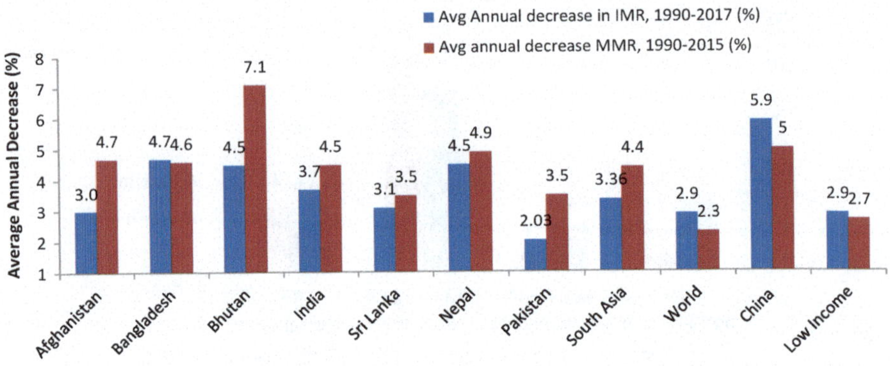

Source: World Development Indicators

Fig. 5.6 Comparison of average annual change in infant mortality rate and maternal mortality ratio: Pakistan and World and select countries

An interesting observation on comparing the trends in IMR and MMR (Fig. 5.6) reveals that Pakistan has made remarkable improvement in reducing MMR over decades, but could not succeed in reducing its IMR to the desired level. Over the entire period during 1990–2015, the annual average decrease in MMR in Pakistan was a meagre 3.5%. In fact, unlike IMR, the annual average decrease in MMR in Pakistan is even larger as compared to the world regions taken together (2.3%) and 2.7% in low-income countries.

Another important health outcome indicator is the life expectancy at birth. Pakistan has been making great improvements in this indicator. Not only has the life expectancy at birth steadily increased, Fig. 5.7 shows that there have been no gender disparities as life expectancy of females has been consistently higher than that of males over the 2007–2017 period.

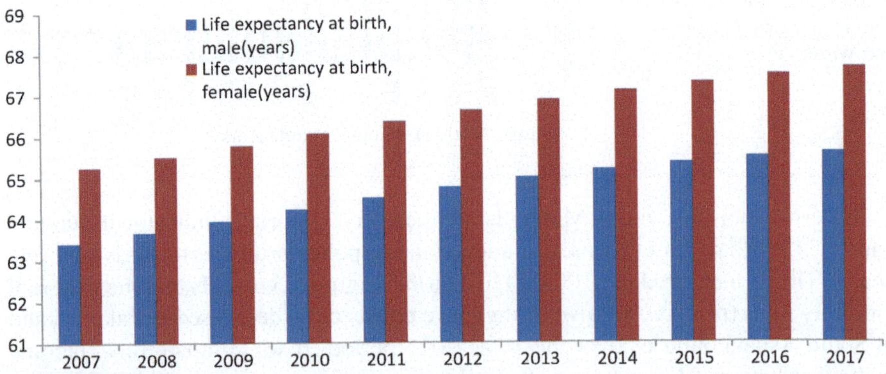

Source: World Development Indicators

Fig. 5.7 Life expectancy at birth (male) vs life expectancy at birth (female), Pakistan

Experimental Health Outcome Index

An experimental health outcome index (HOI) has been computed for Pakistan and emerging economies using life expectancy at birth (LEB), IMR and MMR as indicators. LEB, MMR and IMR figures are from the time period 2017 (latest data available). The health outcome index was computed by standardizing the above indicators. The data reveals that Pakistan has the lowest health outcome index whereas China has the highest. Out of the 14 countries, 10 countries have recorded a health outcome index higher than the world (0.771). Pakistan has a health outcome index marginally lower than the low-income countries (Fig. 5.8).

However, the year-wise health outcomes show a significant improvement for Pakistan (Fig. 5.9). The index calculated for the period 2007–2015 using the same indicators as above shows that health outcome index has increased from 0.413 in 2007 to 0.550 in 2015.

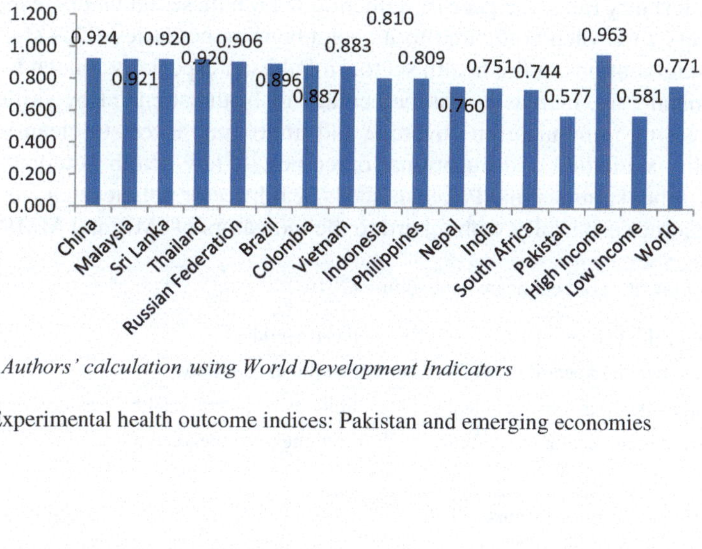

Authors' calculation using World Development Indicators

Fig. 5.8 Experimental health outcome indices: Pakistan and emerging economies

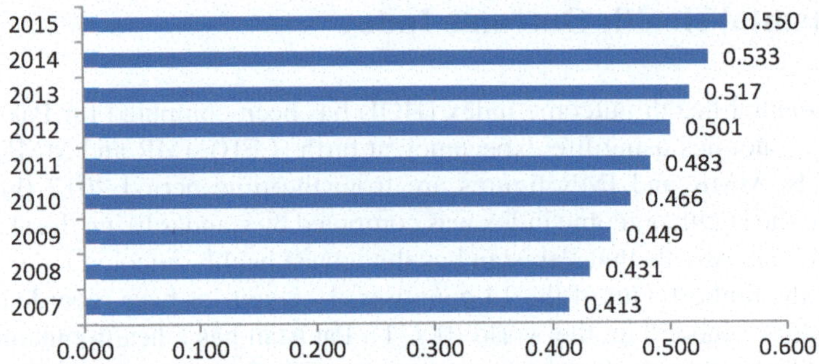

Authors' calculation using World Development Indicators

Fig. 5.9 Experimental health outcome index: Pakistan (2005-2015)

Although the country has achieved gains in reducing its infant mortality and maternal mortality rates, the pace of reduction in both these indicators (especially in IMR) is very low when compared to its neighbouring countries. This signals cost-effective interventions in the health sector in Pakistan especially related to prenatal and post-natal care, increasing the percentage of births attended by skilled health staff, increasing immunization coverage and improving access to clean water and good-quality sanitation and nutritional outcomes. A low health outcome index in Pakistan further signifies that Pakistan needs health sector policies that can improve health outcomes especially with regard to the indicators of IMR and MMR.

Indicators of the level of healthcare expenditure (2016)

1. Current health expenditure as % of gross domestic product	3%
2. Domestic health expenditure as % of current health expenditure	96%
3. Domestic general government health expenditure as % current health expenditure	28%
4. Domestic private health expenditure as % current health expenditure	68%
5. Out-of-pocket expenditure per capita in US $	26%

Source National Health Accounts (NHA)

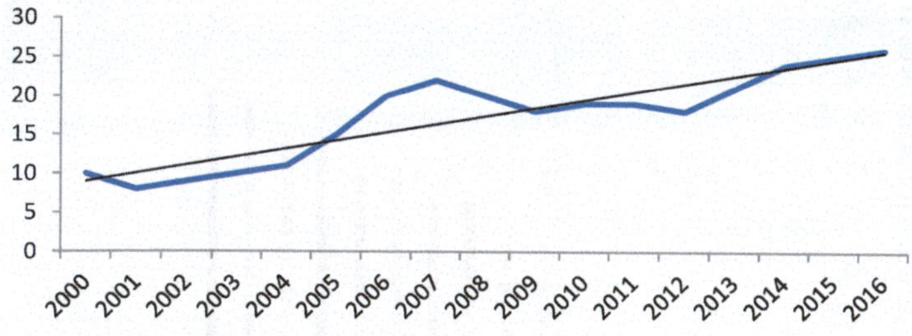

Source: World Development Indicators

Fig. 5.10 Out-of-pocket expenditure (OOPS) per capita in US$

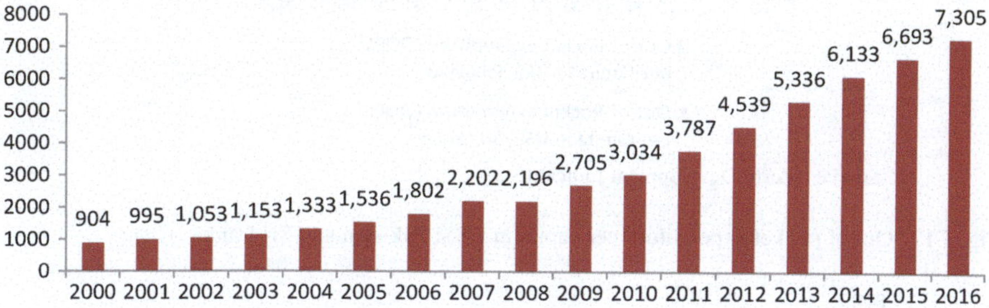

Source: World Development Indicators

Fig. 5.11 Social health insurance schemes(in million NCU), Pakistan

As it is depicted in Fig. 5.10, the out-of-pocket (OOP) expenditure in Pakistan has registered a steady increase from 2000 to 2016. This implies augmenting health inequalities in Pakistan. Although when compared with many of the regional peers for example Sri Lanka, Pakistan is faring better. The per capita out-of-pocket expenditure in Sri Lanka has been consistently higher than in Pakistan. Figure 5.13 further reveals that the expenditure incurred by the respective governments on social health insurance schemes has also been consistently higher in Pakistan (Figs. 5.11 and 5.12).

Health Financing: Recent Direction Towards UHC

Countries including the low–middle and high income are finding innovative ways to design policies in order to meet the newly set SDGs given by the UN, which includes achievements towards Universal Health Coverage (UHC). The WHO 2010 report on health financing documents country-specific cases of health financing measures and also their innovations on that front. It is reported that Pakistan for quite a long time has been taxing the profits of pharmaceutical companies in order to partly finance the health spending. Two major target indicators for designing health financing in any

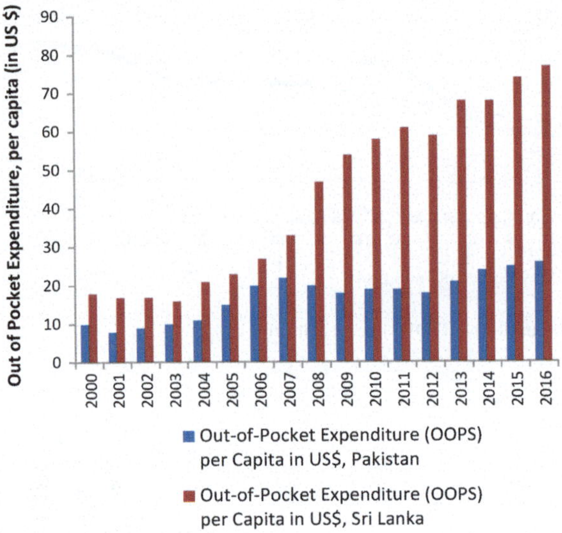

Source: World Development Indicators

Fig. 5.12 Out of pocket expenditure per capita in US$: Pakistan and Sri Lanka

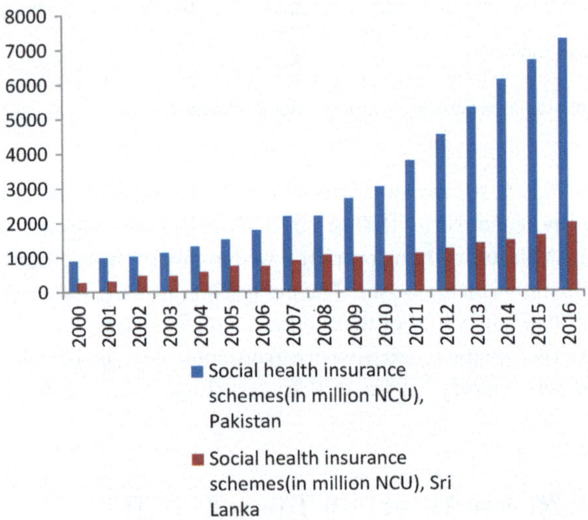

Source: World Development Indicators

Fig. 5.13 Social health insurance schemes (in Million National Currency Units): Pakistan and Sri Lanka

Table 5.1 Trends in select health indicators

Sl. no.	Parameter	2002	2007	2012	2017
1.	Crude birth rate (per 1000 people)	30.8	30.1	29.8	27.7
2.	Crude death rate (per 1000 people)	8.4	8.0	7.6	7.2
3.	Total fertility rate	4.3	3.9	3.7	3.4
4.	Infant mortality rate (per 1000 live births)	84.4	76.9	69.7	61.2
5.	Life expectancy at birth (total)	63.1	64.3	65.7	66.6
6.	Life expectancy at birth (male)	62.4	63.4	64.8	65.6
7.	Life expectancy at birth (female)	64.1	65.3	66.6	67.7

Source World Development Indicators

country while meeting the SDGs are: reducing catastrophic health spending (CHS) and widening health service coverage to include all the citizens. However, insurance is not a very viable option to pool and give protection against CHS for countries that have huge informal sector. This is because payroll taxes are not feasible to be levied in the informal sector where limited job data is available and also due to its huge size the government is often fiscally constrained to cover this sector (Table 5.1).

Pakistan has very recently developed a very innovative model of health financing towards UHC, known as the Heartfile Health Financing (HHF), developed by an NGO in Pakistan. This is widely being discussed in the policy forum and is yet to be implemented (Nishtar et al. 2010). As depicted by the authors, HHF is consisted of three platforms: a technology platform, health equity fund and a system of validating poor and health prioritizing patients. As it has been noted, health is not included in the core instruments of Pakistan's social protection policy that is prevailing. In terms of proportion spent under total health spending, it is only 0.32%. Existing social protection schemes include Zakat and Bait-ul-Mal. In 2007–2008, only 11% allocations of Zakat and 8% of Bait-ul-Mal funds were made. HHF is a demand-side intervention for the most vulnerable in terms of the health indicators and is designed to cater the implementation-related and other associated challenges with the social protection schemes (Table 5.2).

Private sector participation is mostly curative in nature. The CHE is designed by using the rural healthcare network. It has been widely discussed in the policy forum that in order to meet the burgeoning need of the healthcare sector in Pakistan innovative financing mechanism maintaining equity such as user fee or local government-level mobilization of funds is needed to be designed urgently.

Conclusion and Policy Implications

Current healthcare spending in Pakistan is abysmally low as compared to many other low–middle-income peers, close to 2% of GDP or about USD 17 per capita with government's contribution being only a quarter. On the other hand, health outcomes

Table 5.2 Pakistan and emerging economies: select indicators

Country	Under 5 mortality rate (per 1000 live births), year: 2017	Neonatal mortality rate (per 1000 live births), year: 2017	Maternal mortality ratio (per 1,00,000 live births), year: 2015	Life expectancy at birth total (years), year: 2017
Brazil	14.8	8.5	44	75.7.
China	9.3	4.7	27	76.4
Colombia	14.7	8	64	74.5
Indonesia	25.4	12.4	126	69.3
India	39.4	24	174	68.8
Sri Lanka	8.8	5.8	30	75.5
Malaysia	7.9	4.3	40	75.4
Nepal	33.7	20.7	258	70.6
Pakistan	**74.9**	**44.2**	**178**	**66.6**
Philippines	28.1	13.6	114	69.2
Russia	7.6	3.3	25	72.1
South Africa	37.1	10.7	138	63.4
Thailand	9.5	5.3	20	75.5
Vietnam	20.9	10.6	54	76.5
World	**39.1**	**18**	**216**	**72.2**

Source World Development Indicators

are also not satisfactory, and far below the WHO recommended benchmarks. In terms of health outcome indicators like IMR, MMR and life expectancy at birth, Pakistan is lagging behind; although visible improvements are happening with respect to MMR and LEB, high IMR is a cause of concern to the health policy makers. This paper has tried to form an experimental health outcome index. According to the index built, Pakistan is far away from other emerging countries in the region. In order to meet the SDGs, several health financing steps have been taken by the private sector and the government in Pakistan, specially towards UHC and social protection. Although social health insurance schemes have steadily increased in Pakistan, this has not resulted in a commensurate decrease in the out-of-pocket payments by households in Pakistan. On the contrary, the out-of-pocket expenditure in the country has risen. This calls for urgent policy review of the outreach of social health insurance schemes in Pakistan. Probably, the reasons for this could be due to low enrolment owing to low financial literacy and awareness among the marginalized poor and low insurance cover. In recent times, in order to meet the SDGs several innovative health financing steps have been taken by the private sector, NGOs and the government of Pakistan, specially towards UHC and social protection. The paper discusses the new health financing mechanisms such as HHF which are being implemented in phased manner in Pakistan as pilot projects and are recognized widely to be commendable steps towards mobilizing resources and increasing efficiency in health sector financing. If such pilots are found to be successful, these mechanisms can be replicated for other low–middle-income countries as well.

Reference

Nishtar S et al (2010) Protecting the poor against health impoverishment in Pakistan: proof of concept of the potential within innovative web and mobile phone technologies. World Health Report, Background Paper, 55, World Health Organization

Chapter 6
Health Services in Nepal

Bhuban B. Bajracharya

Case Study Nepal

This case study analyzes the trade in health service in South Asia through Nepal's perspective. Nepal is a landlocked least developed country (LDC) in South Asia. The Government of Nepal is cognizant about the benefit of global economic integration. In 2004, the country is acceded to the World Trade Organization (WTO) through the normal process of accession. In the same year, it also joined the regional trading agreements such as the South Asian Free Trade Agreement (SAFTA) and the Bay of Bengal Initiative for Multi-Sectoral Technical and Economic Cooperation (BIM-STEC). Further, the country has a bilateral preferential trade agreement with three countries (Indian, Tibet, and Pakistan).

Against this background, the case study focuses on the status of trade on health services of Nepal with other South Asian countries and analyzes the barriers of smooth flow in such trades. The study primarily focuses on Mode 2 and Mode 3 since Mode 2 is most used one in health trade in the global context (Chanda, op cit.), while FDI inflow through Mode 3 is important in developing countries for investment and technology transfer (Maskay et al. 2006). The study also touches upon the health trade potential through other two modes.

Nepal is a net importer of health services but there are several health services in which country could have comparative advantage. Such potentials are yet to be properly explored and exploited for economic benefits of the country. Further, there is a need to identify the constraints to provide health services through each of these

The authors would like to express their deepest gratitude to the South Asia Network for Economic Institutions (SANEI) in Kathmandu, Nepal for allowing us to use some contents of the Chapter 7 of the report entitled, "Trade in Health Services in South Asia: An Examination of the Need for Regional Cooperation" submitted by the authors.

B. B. Bajracharya (✉)
Freelance Development Economist, Kathmandu, Nepal
e-mail: bbbajracharya@yahoo.com

A. Banik (ed.), *Trade in Health Services in South Asia*,
https://doi.org/10.1007/978-981-15-2191-1_6

modes. So, the study covering a time period of around 2010 has dwelt upon (i) Policy Framework of Nepal in Health Service; (ii) The status of Nepal in term of Health Export and Import; and (iii) Address the constraints on supply of health services via each mode.

This country case study has used both secondary and primary information. For health export status, the study uses the SAWTEE database of 50 foreign patients who had been treated in Nepal in 2007. The other information regarding health trade service has been collected through key informant interview using the checklists.

There is no authentic recording of health service trade in Nepal, and data in all four modes are also not available. Nepal Rastra Bank (Central Bank of Nepal) maintains the record of foreign exchange transaction by purpose which again is underestimated due to substantial informal health trade. So, this country study has tried to present a glance of health trade on the basis of scattered information—some of them collected ones.

The study has the following limitations.

- The study identifies the potential of Nepal's health service trade with South Asia. But it does not analyze the other overlapping trade potential which would be benefited by the enhancement of the health trade.
- The study has conducted the field survey to identify the constraints and barrier to health service import in Nepal. The study is largely based on secondary sources, such as the SAWTEE 2008 database.
- The field survey is limited to about 15 key informants that include doctors, other medical personnel, regulators, private sector, banks, and NGOs.
- The study could not substantially explore Modes 1 and 4 of health service due to this.

Health Services in Nepal—Characteristics and Policy

Policy Framework of Health Services

The health sector services in Nepal are guided by the National Health Policy, 1991, the Second Long-Term Health Plan (SLTHP 1997–2017), and the periodic Development Plans such as the present Three Year Interim Plan (TYIP). While these policies and planning documents guided the strategies as appeared in the "Health Sector Strategy: An agenda for Reform" in 2003 and "Nepal Health Sector Program-Implementation Plan" (NHSP-IP) in 2004, Local Self Governance Act, 1999, spells out the responsibility of the local bodies in health service-related decisions and extension of health services in at the local level.

The public health system covers health services in both rural and urban areas. It is organized as a system of public and private health institutions interlinked through a network of: (i) public hospitals at district, zone, regional, and central level, (ii)

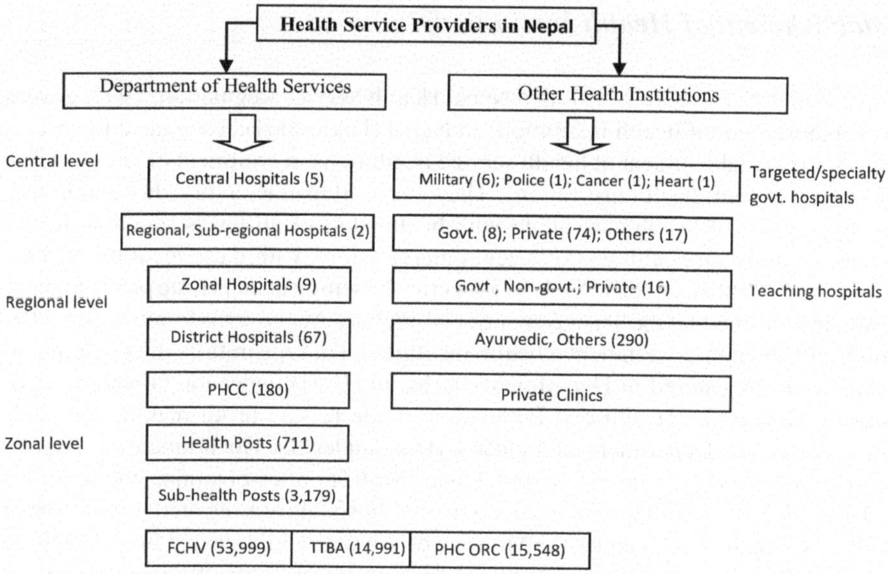

Fig. 6.1 Flowchart of health service provider in Nepal. *Source* http://www.moh.gov.np/Home/FACT.ASP

health posts at VDC and ward level (iii) private health institutions (iv) National Disease-Specific Health Institutions, and (v) Ayurvedic and other traditional health institutions. NHP 1991 has organized the public health system of Nepal from the lower tier to the upper tier as well as categorizing other health institutions (Fig. 6.1). Further, it is important to note how the existing organizational structure of GON's Department of Health Services (DoHS) relates to the different administrative levels as a public health care network as per NHP 1991.

The basic health services are largely provided by the public sector, and the specialized services are covered by both the public and private sector. The non-government sector incorporating "for profit" private institutions, non-governmental organizations (NGOs) and mission hospitals provided 41% of the total beds in 2003 (MOH 2003) and they are mostly concentrated in the urban areas. Together with the liberal policy shift, GON is taking a very proactive approach for the development of the private sector including promoting public–private partnership with particular emphasis on the private sector on tertiary care.[1] Nepal Health Service Act, 2053 BS and Nepal Health Service Rules, 2055 BS are the legal documents to govern the health service in Nepal presently. Six councils are instituted under special laws and regulation of respective councils.

---

[1]TYIP also includes the strategy of managing and coordinating human, financial and physical resources for the quality improvement of the services provided under the partnership of private, government and non-government sector.

Establishment of Health Institutions

Nepal Health Service Act, 1997, and Nepal Health Service Regulation, 1997, govern the establishment of health institutions in Nepal (Dixit 2004). They have the provisions for the establishment of health service institutions, recruitment of health staffs, and supervision of health institutions. They cover allopathic, ayurvedic, and homeopathy streams of health care along with health staff of all levels (doctors, health assistants, assistant health workers, and others). Along with these legal provisions, Industrial Enterprises Act (IEA), 1992, governs the setting up of private profit-making health institutions and the Trust Act or Social Welfare Act governs in setting up other non-profit and non-governmental health institution. For registration, the government hospitals are registered in Department of Health (DoH) under the Government of Nepal's Ministry of Health and Population, while private profit-making hospitals are registered in Department of Industry (DoI) under the Government of Nepal's Ministry of Industry, Commerce and Trade (MoICT) after obtaining the approval of DoH. The non-profit and non-governmental hospitals are registered with Social Welfare Council (SWC) under the Ministry of Women, Children and Social Welfare (MoWCSW) after getting the consent of DoH. Some disease-specific hospitals owned by government are also established under their own specific acts. For instance, B. P. Koirala Memorial Cancer Hospital has been established under B.P. Koirala Memorial Cancer Hospital Act, 1997, and Shaheed Ganga Lal National Heart Center has been established under the Shaheed Ganga Lal National Heart Centre Act, 1997. After registration in concerned department, the health institution needs to be registered at Inland Revenue Office to obtain a Permanent Account Number (PAN) and obtain permission for trademarks, patents, and designs if necessary.

Foreign Direct Investment and Health Services

Foreign Investment and Technology Transfer Act (FITTA), 1992, regulates the FDI in health sector under which FDI inflow needs to be registered with the Department of Investment after the approval from DoI, DoH, and Company Registrar's Office (CRO). Foreign investors are required to undergo through the steps of (i) incorporating at CRO; (ii) registering and obtaining approval from DoI and DoH; and (iii) registering and getting approval from the Department of Investment. As there is no clear documentation on the FDI approval procedure, the approval is granted case by case. To facilitate the above-mentioned procedures, though there is One Window Committee (OWC) at the MoICT of Government of Nepal, it is less functional. Foreign investors can own up to 100% equity in private health firms and are entitled to repatriate the investment amount and other earnings. Further, to facilitate business transactions, foreign exchange restrictions are relaxed. Likewise, there is a provision for business visas for foreign investors for up to 5 years. Provisions also exist for providing non-tourist visas to carry out studies for investment along with residential visas for foreign investors.

Qualification and Licensing Criteria of Medical Practitioner

Nepal Medical Council (NMC) established under the Nepal Medical Council Act (NMCA) is the responsible body to regulate and maintain the standard of the medical and dental doctors in Nepal. Likewise, Nepal Nursing Council established under Nepal Nursing Council Act is responsible body to regulate and maintain the standard of the nurses and assistant health workers. These councils are responsible to recognize the medical certificates of concerned health personnel and supervise the medical teaching institutions. In South Asia, NMC has recognized more than 116 medical degrees (MBBS and postgraduate) 6 from Bangladeshi universities, over 100 from the Indian universities, 9 from Pakistani universities, and 1 from Sri Lankan university. NMCA also allows foreign medical professional to practice in Nepal for one year after getting permission of NMC.

Provision of Visa for People's Movement

Visa provision is one of the most important factors for the Indians. It is not required for them. The residents of countries other than India can apply for three months tourist visa in the Nepali embassy of the country of residence and extend such visa for another three months. If there is no Nepali embassy in the country of residence, then the applicant can apply for free visa for three days at the border entry points and receive the tourist visa from Department of Immigration within these three days.

Nepal's Commitment in GATS

In terms of the country's general commitment in service sector, the market access limitation of Nepal includes: (i) convertible currency limit of USD 2000 which is applied to Nepalese citizens on personal travel under Mode 2, (ii) none would be made more restrictive than that of date accession under mode three, and (iii) For mode four "Unbound," except for temporary entry and stay of natural persons of another Member as Service salespersons, Persons responsible for setting up a commercial presence and Intra-corporate transferees. Nepal is silent on Mode 1 under the market access limitation. The limitation on National Treatment includes: (i) None, except with respect to foreign exchange provided to foreigners (excluding those categories of persons covered by commitments in this agreement) to pay for any cross-border

Table 6.1 Nepal's health sector commitment in GATS

Sector or sub-sector	Limitation in market access	Limitations on national treatment
Health-related and social services A. Hospital services (CPC 9311) and direct ownership and management by contract of such facilities on a 'for fee' basis	1. None 2. None 3. None, except only through incorporation in Nepal and with maximum foreign equity capital of 51% 4. Unbound, except as indicated in the horizontal section Medical experts can work with the permission of Nepal Medical Council for maximum of one year	1. None 2. None 3. None 4. Unbound, except as indicated in the horizontal section

Source WTO Web site

services for Mode one; (ii) None for Mode 2; (iii) None except approval from concern department for mode three; and (iv) Unbound except for measures concerning the categories of natural persons referred to in the market access column for mode four. Nepal has also made an additional general commitment in terms of environmental impact and repatriate. Nepal has made a specific commitment only in hospital services. The specific commitments in hospital services are given in Table 6.1.

FDI cap of 51% in GATS is a binding international commitment. However, the country has more liberal FDI policy of unilaterally allowing the cap of 100% in FDI in hospital.

International Trade in Health Services

NRB study shows that the health service accounts for nominal share in the service trade of Nepal—only 0.8% in 2004.[2] However, FDI flow is expanding—28.2% of total FDI flow in service sector in 2004 (NRB 2005). Nepal Rastra Bank data suggest that Nepal is a net importer of the health treatment services in terms of modes one and two on aggregate, and there is also an increasing trend in FDI approval.

As per the key informant interviews, the major diseases for which health services are exported and imported are provided in Table 6.2. The Nepalese patients of cancer, neuro, kidney, liver, and heart generally travel to foreign countries particularly to India for treatment. On the other hand, the Indian residents near to the border come to hospitals located in Terai region of Nepal for treatment. Basically, they come to Nepal for the services related to pathology, general medicine, and gastroenterology.

[2]Tourism is the dominant sector contributing one-third of the total trade in services and one-half of the total FDI flow in service sector in Nepal.

Table 6.2 Major diseases with import and export of health services in Nepal

Major disease and related health services that Nepali received in foreign land	Major diseases and related health services that foreign individuals received in Nepal
• Cancer • Neuro-related diseases • Kidney-related diseases • Liver-related disease • Heart-related disease	• Pathology (In Terai Belt) • General Medicine (In Terai Belt) • Gastroenterology (In Terai Belt) • Eye • Ayurvedic treatment

Source Key informant interview

Further, Nepal also exports health services in eye-related diseases and Ayurvedic treatment.

Mode 1: The recent rapid development in information and communication technologies and health informatics has dramatically changed the picture. Telemedicine, the practice of medical care using interactive audio, visual, and data communications, includes medical care delivery, consultations, diagnosis and treatment, as well as the transfer of medical data. In the key informant interview with an official from the Nick Simon Institution, it was learnt that there are all together around 25 hospitals in Nepal that are providing telemedicine facilities and all of them are either government funded or charity hospital. Om Hospital was the only private hospital that had once initiated this service but later discontinued. However, there are no other health service institutions in Nepal providing telemedicine facilities to the patients in foreign countries.

Mode 2: Nepal has a substantial outflow of patients to foreign countries especially India as Nepal has limited capacity in providing services for many diseases. In the key informant interview with senior doctors and medical professionals, it came out that the major diseases for which Nepal is not adequately equipped are cancer, neuro-related diseases, kidney-related diseases, and liver-related diseases. The information collected from the field survey and other secondary sources show a significant number of patients going out to other countries for treatment (Table 6.3).

As for inflow of patients from foreign countries, a significant number of Indian patients visit Nepal for health care. The patients are generally from low-income groups with their mean income around IRs. 7000. It could mean that the country does not offer or the patients do not perceive expensive high-quality specialized health services available in the country (Table 6.4).

Eye care service providers have some strategies to export the services for consumers of different levels of income. For example, eye hospital at Biratnagar has several choices for the consumer for cataract services—ranging from NRs. 900, 1700, 2500, 3500, 5000 and to 8000. However, Koshi and BPKIHS are able to provide only very limited choices. Choices are limited in terms of both service levels mainly addressing to different income brackets and health service providers. Due to this, they divert to the Patna and Darbhanga for consumption of health services. Nepalese institutions could provide services for the low- and middle-income groups.

Table 6.3 Outflow of patients from Nepal to foreign countries

Source of information	Flow of patient	Remarks
Bajracharya and Bajracharya (2008)	Average of 2–3 Patients per day to Indian Cities	Migrant Movement Survey conducted in Nepalgunj and Danghadhi (Two Bordering Cities with India in Mid and Far Western Region of Nepal) using Purposive Sampling of 25 respondent collected in 2 days
Handicap International (2008)	Average of 9–11 patient per day to Indian Cities	Migrant movement survey conducted in Bairahawa (Bordering Cities of with India in Central Region of Nepal) using purposive sampling of 100 respondents collected in 4 days
Hospital agents (Apollo Hospital, Delhi; Bangkok Hospital, Bangkok)[a]	Average 4–5 patient go to Bangkok and Apollo Hospital for treatment	Collected by study team during key informant interview
Cancer patient association of Nepal[a]	In last three years, average of 8–10 patients per year consult the association regarding procedure to treat in different Indian Cities	Collected by study team during key informant interview
Nepal Kidney Association[a]	In last year, average of 4 patient went to India for treatment	

[a]Collected during key informant interview

Table 6.4 General characteristics of Indian patients coming to Nepal for health services

Statistics	Age	Years of schooling	Monthly income (IRS)	Persons accompanied with the patients
Mean	41	5	7390.74	3
Median	45	4	5550.00	3
Mode	60	1	3000.00	2
Std. Deviation	20	4	8938.43	1
Minimum	1	1	1500	0
Maximum	80	16	30,000	8

Source SAWTEE (2008)

Table 6.5 Foreign direct investment in health services

Category	Number of firms	Foreign investment (Rs. in million)	Local employment	Foreign employment
Operating	7	1617	877	138
Approved	4	1445	1524	1531
Total	11	3062	2401	1669

Maskay et al. (2006)

Mode 3: There are moderate flows of FDI in the health sector in Nepal. The first (a Nursing home with Chinese FDI) was granted permission for operation in 1991. In 2005, the FDI of the seven operating firms total about Rs. 1.6 billion (approximately US$ 231 million) and the four firms have been approved by the government of Nepal and are in the course of operation (Table 6.5).

Mode 4: There is a regular flow of Indian specialists visiting Nepal to provide specialized services to the Nepalese patients through private hospitals and nursing homes in Nepal. Further, there are a substantial number of foreign medical professionals coming to Nepal as visiting professors (SAWTEE 2008).

Barriers to Health Services Exports

Major problems expressed by the clients/patients from outside the country receiving health services in Nepal during the field survey include (i) absence of ward facilities and (ii) lack of the adequate information on the service providers and limited choices of service providers. A few respondents mentioned security problems/unpredictable situation in the country and also cheating in the transportation (particularly by the taxis in the Kathmandu Valley). Though the study could not capture non-Indian foreigners, service providers themselves informed that they usually face additional problem of limited choices in food items.

With regard to movement of the patients, one of the most important barriers is emotional insecurity of patients who do not wish to be far from their families and are particularly sensitive of possible cultural and linguistic differences. However, the patients from India did not face any such problems including language, discrimination in providing consultation services, and cultural both within and beyond the service providers while receiving health services in Nepal. Disincentives for the export of health services from the service providers' perspective have been elaborated as follows.

Mode 1: Telemedicine is in practice in a limited way. However, quality of such services is yet up to the mark for several reasons—major being limited professional capacity and need for huge investment.

Mode 2: Patients particularly from India come for (i) specialized and surgical treatments, specially eye care that employ advanced technology which may not be available at home; (ii) less expensive (in terms of time and money) services. However, lack of or incomplete information is likely to limit the flow of patients to Nepal.

The availability of health services with various facilities and fee levels attract patients from different income levels. It is particularly so for eye care.

Eye hospital in Biratnagar provides cataract operation at fee ranging from Nrs. 900, to Nrs. 8000. But such choice is often limited. Choices are limited in terms of both range of facilities for the same services and service providers. Due to this, patients from India tend to go to Patna and Darbhanga for health services, and the Nepalese institutions provide services for the low- and middle-income groups.

Mode 3: The health sector is also open for foreign investment and competition from abroad. However, the continued political instability and highly income elastic nature of the demand, there is not much incentive for such investment at the moment.

Mode 4: There is debate on how to get benefit from the outflow of health personnel. The outflow of health personnel has a clear impact on equity if it produces shortages in the home country, thus reducing access to the services that would have been provided by the migrant health personnel. The loss of specific categories of health professionals will also reduce the range of services available. On the other hand, if the categories of health personnel involved are those in which the home country has an oversupply, then, in that case, the country can get benefit from exporting those skilled health personnel. Lack of clear-cut vision with regard to the outflow of health personnel such as cost–benefit analysis is limiting the access of market in this mode.

Finally, lack of awareness of our own potential areas for exporting health services and lack of policy priority for promoting trade in the health sector are also responsible elements working as disincentive in this sector.

Reforms and Potential Benefits

The trade of health services offers various benefits to the country–new market opportunities, foreign exchange, and discouraging migration of qualified health personnel.

Various international driving forces are exerting a significant influence on health services and are creating opportunities in the health sector. Health is an essential good that can be linked with other sectors such as tourism and education. Studies have identified different channels of potential benefit depending on the country context. In the Chilean context, such specifics are identified inprioritizing elder care, establishing the links between tourism and health, exporting health service to border areas, enhancing international agreements on health insurances, and facilitating specialized professional and technical training. Similarly, for India, they are in identified (1) upgradation of basic amenities and hospital infrastructure, (2) coordination between the healthcare and tourism sectors, (3) creating a resource pool of highly skilled and cordial manpower, (4) standardization of services and accreditation of hospitals, (5) increasing visibility of India on the world map, and (6) the impact on domestic healthcare services as the issues requiring attention with reference to medical tourism. The channels which are practiced presently are appropriate or not for future in order to exploit the potential export opportunities for Nepal are discussed below.

Channels for First Mode

Advancement in telemedicine and the Internet have led to new opportunities for exporting health services worldwide. The practice of telemedicine addresses a number of issues, including cost containment, optimizing the use of expensive technology and specialized medical services, upgrading of health treatment, improving access of patients in remote areas to primary and specialized health services, and regional sharing of knowledge and cooperation. This facilitates international flow of the service usually from more advanced location to less advanced areas. However, in Nepal, in the absence of reliable communication infrastructure and of proper coordination and integration with the foreign health service providers, problems remain with quality assurance, reliability, and competitive cost structure. Hence, in brief, there remains less feasibility to export significant services in the present context via first mode in Nepal.

Channels for Second Mode

To expand the exports via second mode, areas of both competitive and comparative advantages should be considered. Currently, following elements have been working as the important elements for exporting the services.

- Inexpensive health services: Health services are available at lower (affordable) cost in Nepal compared to Bihar and Uttar Pradesh.
- Regular campaigns: Particularly eye hospitals of Nepal are regularly conducting campaign in rural communities in India.
- Establishment of referral chain: Trainings about the symptoms of eye diseases are provided to the representative persons in the communities and are identified as the referral person for eye care in Nepal. Referral chains in the Indian communities have been developed though not formally but are well established.
- Components of comparative/competitive advantages: Different components such as quality, lower travel time, lower cost of treatment, relatives living in Nepal (time, quality, and price) are jointly contributing to the comparative/competitive advantage for attracting patients in Nepal.
- Presence of doctors from India: Some health service providers have Indian doctors.

Potential channels that could be promoted in the future to enhance export of health services by attracting foreign patients are as follows.

- Developing new and unique methods of service delivery that are feasible in the country,
- Integrating health services and tourism,
- Enhancing capacity of the existing service providers where there is greater flow of the foreigners and encouraging for the establishment of other service providers in the nearby locations.

Channels for Third Mode

UNCTAD (1997) has identified a role for developing countries to work with the least developed countries (LDCs) to strengthen their capacity to provide specialized health services to their populations by procuring required modern medical and surgical equipment and training physicians and surgeons in delivering these specialized services. Affiliation or partnership with reputed service providers in advanced countries would enhance service facilities in developing countries by improving quality of services and promoting research and development. Maskay et al. (2006) has examined the practices of service sector investment liberalization and incentives from selected developing countries. He has found that there is no clear relationship between the incentives (e.g., liberalization strategy) and FDI flows; For Nepal, exporting service through outflow of the FDI seems a bit difficult until now which however should not be overlooked for the future. Some of the channels for exporting services through the third mode could be as follows:

- Encouraging recognized specialty service providers to take initiation for extending their services in the foreign market by FDI outflow after ensuring their quality and reviewing comparative cost structure.
- Provisioning regular visit of the medical personnel through management contract or tie up with foreign hospitals at greater number of hospitals in the country.
- Liberalizing the policies of licensing provisions and the establishment of joint venture hospitals,
- Attracting inflow of FDI that has capacity to enhance the export of services through other channels. For example, liberal provisions can be made for attracting reputed foreign hospitals, retirement homes, and old age care centers to made investment in the domestic country that targets to attract service consumers from the foreign land.

Channels for Fourth Mode

As discussed in the earlier section, there is trend of outflow of health personnel usually from developing to developed countries which is the apparent potentiality for the country like Nepal to export service via fourth mode. However, the problem associated with this is that there is also inadequacy of skilled personnel in the country. Together with solving the domestic problems, we can promote the export through the channels as pointed out below.

- Prioritizing the production of medical personnel in the country,
- Promoting bilateral and multilateral agreements for mutual benefits by creating the environment for the movement of natural persons,
- Enhancing international network by coordinating reputed foreign health institutions so as to expand and manage the outflow of health personnel to provide health services in the foreign land.

Nevertheless, Maskay (2004) has highlighted some of the challenges with unbridled liberalization in general, and for Nepal in particular. Likewise, there are a number of barriers which impede the movement of service suppliers, including visa and entry provisions, and licensing and recognition of qualifications which to some extent have been addressed under the GATS. Similarly, at the multilateral level, there is a need for the promotion of transparency in standards and qualifications requirements.

Conclusions and Policy Recommendations

This study makes some observations and recommendations basing on Nepal case study. Health services at most of the public institutions in Nepal are subsidized by the government and services are generally provided from public good perspective. This implies that such public institutions are less important from the trade viewpoint. Therefore, greater involvement of the private sector particularly in operating teaching hospitals and tertiary care, and liberalization of the policies for exporting health services are necessary for exporting the services.

Most of the patients arrived in Nepal from India belong to low-income households. Some patients have expressed their willingness to pay even higher fees for the services; however, they were referring to arrange additional and fringe benefits while consuming the health services. Therefore, provision of at least two or three levels of fee structure with differing facilities particularly at specialty and high-cost treatment providers should be arranged to attract high-income foreign people for service consumption. Rather than the general services, Indian patients are found to be interested in the specialty and chronic problem-related services. Therefore, Indian patients-targeted departments with relevant services should be established particularly in the hospitals which are nearer to India. In doing so, priority should be given to the illness requiring high-cost treatment so that volume of the trade would be large.

Effective information channel needs to be developed to attract larger flow of the patients from the foreign land. Many patients are facing problems in identifying appropriate service provider because of the non-availability of the information regarding available services and the cost structure in different institutions.

It is noted by the study that a different stratum of patients can be attracted in Nepalese hospitals if some unique features can be incorporated in the domestic service system. For this purpose, more focus should be given on research activates for exploring the locally available natural resources that are useful in the treatment and at the same time for developing country-specific unique method of treatment and promoting traditional methods of treatment. Quality of the services is one of the most important elements to attract patients in a particular health institution. Therefore, Nepal government should make necessary provisions for assuring quality of the health services.

Some of the advanced countries such as USA, Canada have high demand for low-cost health service providers, particularly from developing countries. To fulfill this gap in those countries and for the promotion of service export through the bilateral agreements, efforts should be done to attract FDI to raise the production of human resources in the domestic country. By this means, export of health service can be facilitated mainly via mode 4.

Despite the increasing inflow of non-Indian tourists, health tourism is found virtually limited to Indian service consumers in Nepal. Therefore, there is need to integrate health services with the tourism for exporting services to non-Indian foreigners via second mode. For this purpose, gradually, tourists can be attracted for the treatment purpose in the country by making them familiar with the domestic service system through the arrangement of health services in the tour package, etc.

Management tie up and the expansion of the network of the domestic service providers with the reputed foreign health service providers and insurance companies are important for exporting services via both second and third modes. The Nepalese Government can encourage for this primarily through policy adjustments. In the present context of increasing role played by the private sector, the purpose of regulating the health services in the country and registering medical practitioners according to their qualifications by establishing a Medical Council as provisioned in Nepal Medical Council Act seems relevant. Initiation should be taken in this line to ensure quality services and bring homogeneity in the services which are important elements to attract foreign patients for service consumption.

We advocate following recommendations based on our Nepal case study,

- **Encouraging Greater Involvement of Private Sector**: Health services at most of the public institutions in Nepal are subsidized by the government, and services are generally provided from public goods perspective. This implies that such public institutions are less important from the trade viewpoint. Therefore, greater involvement of the private sector particularly in operating teaching hospitals and tertiary care, and liberalization of the policies for exporting health services are necessary for exporting the services.

- **Facility Differentiating at Cost Differentiation**: Most of the patients arrived from India belong to low-income households. However, some patients have expressed their willingness to pay even higher fees for the services. They were referring to arrange additional and fringe benefits while using the health services. Therefore, provision of at least two or three levels of fee structure with differing facilities particularly at specialty and high-cost treatment providers could be arranged to attract high-income foreign people for health services.
- **Promoting Specialty Services**: Rather than the general services, Indian patients are found to be interested in the specialty and chronic problem-related services. Therefore, Indian patients-targeted departments with relevant services should be established particularly in the hospitals which are nearer to India. In doing so, priority should be given to the illness requiring high-cost treatment so that volume of the trade would be large.
- **Building Effective Information Channel**: Effective information channel needs to be developed to attract larger flow of the patients from the foreign land. Many patients are facing problems in identifying appropriate service providers because of the non-availability of the information regarding available services and their cost structure.
- **Promoting Unique Treatment System**: A different strata of patients can be attracted if the unique features can be incorporated in the health service system of the country. For this purpose, more focus should be given on research on exploring the locally available natural resources that are useful in the treatment and at the same time for developing country-specific unique method of treatment and promoting traditional methods of treatment.
- **Assuring of the Service Quality**: Quality of the services is one of the most important elements to attract patients. Therefore, government should make necessary provisions for assuring quality of the health services.
- **Attracting Foreign Investment for Human Resource Development**: Some of the advanced countries, like USA, Canada, have high demand for low-cost health service providers, particularly from developing countries. To fulfill this gap in those countries and for the promotion of service export through the bilateral agreements, efforts should be done to attract FDI to raise the production of human resources in the home country. By this means, export of health service can be facilitated mainly via fourth mode.
- **Integrating Health Services with Tourism Industry**: Despite the increasing inflow of non-Indian tourists, health tourism is found virtually limited to Indian service consumers in Nepal. Therefore, there is a need to integrate health services with the tourism for exporting services to non-Indian foreigners via second mode. For this purpose, gradually tourists can be attracted for the treatment purpose in the country by making them familiar with the service system through the arrangement of health services in the tour package, etc.
- **Management Tie Up and Network Expansion**: Management tie up and the expansion of the network of the domestic service providers with the reputed foreign health service providers and insurance companies are important for exporting

services via both second and third modes. Government can encourage for this primarily through policy adjustments.

- **Effective Policy and Regulatory Provisions**: In the present context of increasing role played by the private sector, the purpose of regulating the health services in the country and registering medical practitioners according to their qualifications by establishing a Medical Council as provisioned in Nepal Medical Council Act seems relevant. Initiation should be taken in this line to ensure quality services and bring homogeneity in the services which are important elements to attract foreign patients for health services.

References

Bajracharya BB, Bajracharya R (2008) Endline evaluation of the community based trafficking prevention initiatives project. Submitted to save the children. Technical Review Group Pvt. Ltd., Kathmandu

Dixit H (2004) Health in Quest: Nepal. Kathmandu

Handicap International (2008) Situation of physically disable in central Terai of Nepal. Kathmandu

Maskay NM (2004) The interaction of increased trade and the decentralization of health care delivery in nepal: a Suggestion for Reform. Yale J Policy, Law, Ethics 4(2)

Maskay NM, Panta RK, Sharma BP (2006) Foreign investment liberalization and incentives in selected Asia-Pacific developing Countries: implications for the health service sector in Nepal. Working paper series, no. 22, Asia-Pacific Research and Training Network on Trade. http://www.unescap.org/tid/artnet

Ministry of Health (2003) Strategic plan for human resources for health 2003 to 2017. Government of Nepal, Kathmandu

Nepal Rastra Bank (2005) Nepal's WTO service sector commitments and its impact on balance of payment situation. Kathmandu, Nepal

SAWTEE (2008) Nepal's export potential in services: health, education and high-end retail services. Kathmandu

UNCTAD (1997) Report of the expert meeting on strengthening the capacity and expanding exports of developing countries in the services sector: health services. UNCTAD

Chapter 7
India: Emerging as Major Destination of Quality Healthcare Services

Arindam Banik and Pradip K. Bhaumik

Analysis of Primary Data

Profile of Patients

A survey of 190 patients who had come to India from other South Asian countries to avail of medical services was conducted during the period of 1914–1915 to understand the trade-related barriers and their effect on actual patients. This chapter captures the essential aspects of the survey.

Tables 7.1 and 7.2 present a socio-demographic and socio-economic profile of the patients. We can see that an overwhelming majority (about 79.5%) of the patients is male and more than half are in the age group 40–59. Not so surprisingly, about 95.8% of the patients are from Bangladesh and about 61.0% of these foreign patients have studied up to SSC/HSC or above.

The largest number of patients is from single earning member households, and for such households, the average number of dependents is 4.97. It must be very difficult for such households to travel to another country for the treatment of one of its members—particularly when we also observe that the average income per household for such households is only 235623.40 in local currency (which effectively means Bangladesh Taka). For double-income households, the average number of dependents

The authors would like to express their deepest gratitude to the South Asia Network for Economic Institutions (SANEI) in Kathmandu, Nepal for allowing us to use some contents of the Chapter 7 of the report entitled, "Trade in Health Services in South Asia: An Examination of the Need for Regional Cooperation" submitted by the authors.

A. Banik (✉)
International Management Institute, Kolkata, India

P. K. Bhaumik (✉)
International Management Institute, New Delhi, India
e-mail: pkbhaumik@imi.edu

A. Banik (ed.), *Trade in Health Services in South Asia*,
https://doi.org/10.1007/978-981-15-2191-1_7

Table 7.1 Socio-demographic profile of sample patients (nos.)

Age categories (years)	Patients			Marital status				Education						
	Male	Female	Total	Unmarried	Married	Widowed	Sptd/Divorced	Cannot read/ write	Can read/write	Some schlg (Up to 4 yrs)	5–9 yrs of school	SSC/HSC	Tech Trg (fml/infml)	Others
Juvenile upto 19	9	6	15	15	0	0	0	7	1	3	4	0	0	0
Youth 20–39	42	17	59	14	45	0	0	1	2	2	9	27	3	15
Middle-aged 40–59	84	15	99	5	94	0	0	0	8	11	20	46	3	11
Old 60 yrs and above	16	1	17	0	17	0	0	1	2	1	2	5	4	2
Total	151	39	190	34	156	0	0	9	13	17	35	78	10	28

Age categories (years)	Countries						
	1	2	3	4	5	6	7
Juvenile upto 19	0	15	0	0	0	0	0
Youth 20–39	0	55	1	0	1	1	1
Middle-aged 40–59	2	96	0	0	1	0	0
Old 60 yrs and above	0	16	0	0	0	0	1
Total	2	182	1	0	2	1	2

Countries: 1—Afghanistan, 2—Bangladesh, 3—Bhutan, 4—Maldives, 5—Nepal, 6—Pakistan, 7—Sri Lanka

Table 7.2 Socio-economic profile of sample patients

Number of earning household members (including respondent)	No. of patients	Adults	Children	Total members	No. of dependents	Average income per household per annum in Taka (for Bangladesh patients only)
0	2	2	2	4	NA	375,000
1	94	335	132	467	4.97	235419.56
2	61	281	107	388	3.18	502965.58
3	17	118	38	156	3.06	691,875
4	8	77	26	103	3.22	495714.28
5	6	55	14	69	2.30	1,060,000
6	2	29	11	40	3.33	890,000

per earning member is 3.18, but the average income per household is about 500,000 units of local currency.

Figure 7.1 shows the source of household income for the sample patients. The largest number of patients (87 out of 190 or 46%) is self-employed followed by another 30% in private service. About 12% have agriculture as their source of income. Surprisingly, about 10% of the patients are in government service in their respective country which implies a perceived lack of medical facilities even for government servants.

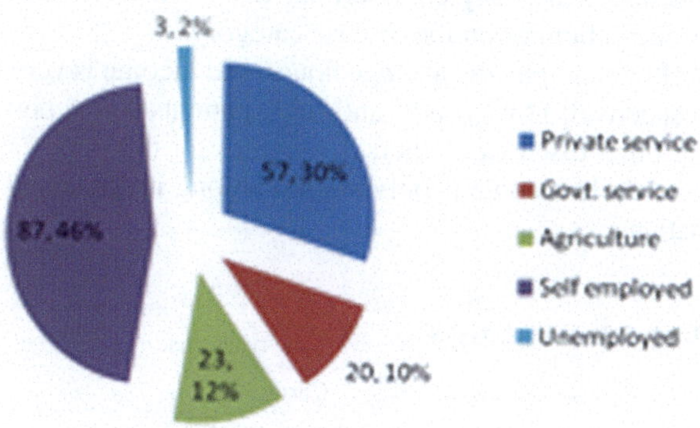

Fig. 7.1 Income source distribution

Profile of Diseases

Table 7.3 reveals that the largest number of patients is coming to India for cardiac (49) and cancer (45) treatment. Orthopaedic (21) and kidney-related (22) treatment also forms a significant percentage of the sample of foreign patients.

Table 7.4 shows the age-wise distribution of diseases among the sample patients. We notice a little bi-modality among cardiology patients—both juvenile (under 19) and middle-aged patients outnumber youth in the sample. The dominance of males across all age groups and across all disease categories is also clearly visible—the only exception being patients who are between 20 and 39 years old and do not have any of the stated diseases. This could be due to gynaecological problems faced by the female youth patients.

Figures 7.2a–d show the disease distribution of patients under different age groups. We find that 80% of the juvenile patients are cardiology patients, whereas there is no such clear dominance among the youth patients—the highest percentage of patients in this age group is from the disease category "others". Cancer is the most common disease among middle-aged patients, and cardiology is the cause for treatment in India for 44% of old patients.

The disease distribution shown in Fig. 7.3 suggests that cardiology and cancer seem to be the diseases for which most of the patients are coming to India. However, a gender-wise reclassification shows that while cardiology is a common disease among both male and female patients, cancer is not that common a disease among female patients. In fact, Fig. 7.4a, b shows different disease profiles for male and female patients.

In Table 7.5, we analyse the average household income of Bangladesh patients under different age groups and undergoing treatment for different types of diseases. We do not find any common pattern for household income based either on the age of the patient or on the disease category.

For example, the average household income is very high (1,680,000 and 785,530, respectively) for "youth" and "old" patients who reported to be undergoing treatment for other diseases ("others"), whereas for the same category of disease, the average household income is only 40,000 among juvenile and 310,400 among middle-aged patients.

Table 7.3 Disease types

Type of disease	No. of patients
Cardiology	49
Orthopaedics	21
Ophthalmology	6
Cancer	45
Kidney related	22
Neurology	11
Others	36

Table 7.4 Age-wise distribution of patients

Age (years completed)	Type of disease	No. of patients	Male	Female
Juvenile upto 19	Cardiology	12	7	5
	Ophthalmology	1	0	1
	Kidney related	1	1	0
	Others	1	1	0
Youth 20–39	Cardiology	7	5	2
	Orthopaedics	12	12	0
	Ophthalmology	2	1	1
	Cancer	7	4	3
	Kidney related	9	9	0
	Neurology	3	2	1
	Others	19	9	10
Middle-aged 40–59	Cardiology	23	18	5
	Orthopaedics	8	7	1
	Ophthalmology	2	1	1
	Cancer	34	31	3
	Kidney related	11	10	1
	Neurology	6	5	1
	Others	15	12	3
Old 60 yrs and above	Cardiology	7	7	0
	Orthopaedics	1	0	1
	Ophthalmology	1	1	0
	Cancer	4	4	0
	Kidney related	1	1	0
	Neurology	2	2	0
	Others	1	1	0

Disease Diagnosis and Treatment

Figure 7.5 reveals that the vast majority of patients got their diagnosis done in their home country. Apparently, the local doctors advised them to go abroad for better treatment in view of insufficient facilities and expertise in the home country.

Not only was the diagnosis done in home country; in many cases, we find that the patient knew about the disease diagnosis, but could not come earlier due to lack of resources as revealed in Fig. 7.6. These could be both financial and non-financial. Many non-financial resources may be employed to overcome the different barriers to trade in health services.

Figure 7.7 shows that there is positive correlation between the annual household income and the amount spent on medical treatment in India, although the slope of the

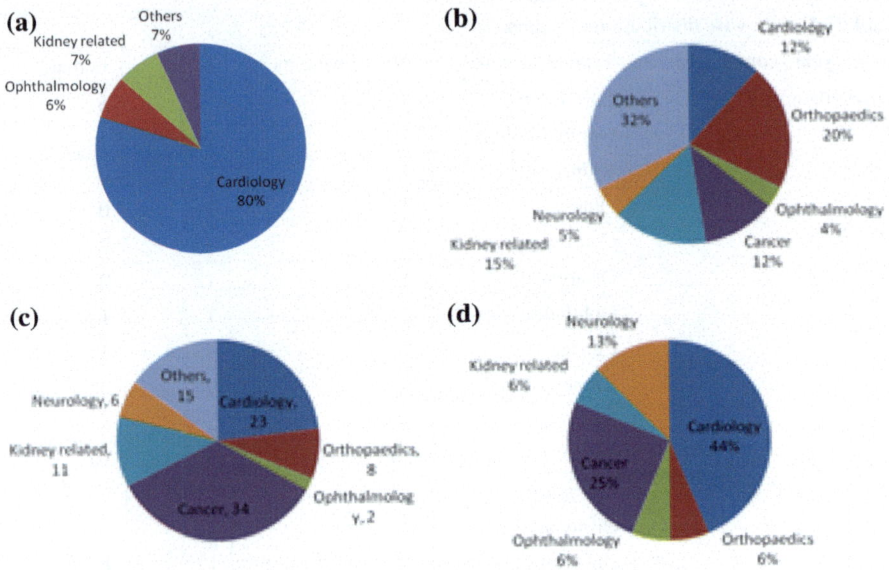

Fig. 7.2 Patients distribution under the age group **a** up to 19 years, **b** 20–39 years, **c** 40–59 years and **d** 60 years and above

Fig. 7.3 Reporting diseases

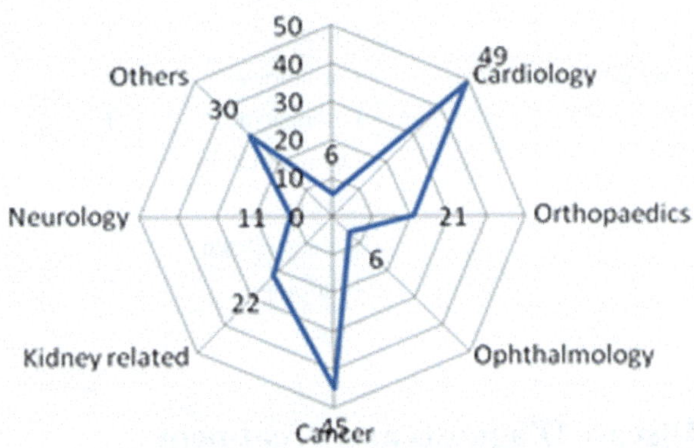

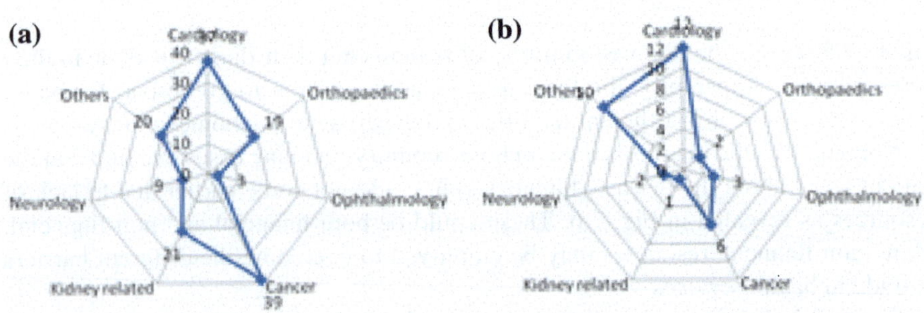

Fig. 7.4 **a** Reporting diseases among males and **b** reporting diseases among females

Table 7.5 Disease and economic characteristics of Bangladesh patients

Age (years completed)	Type of disease	No. of patients	Avg. income (in Bangladesh Taka)
Juvenile upto 19	Cardiology	12	276,833
	Ophthalmology	1	100,000
	Kidney related	1	120,000
	Others	1	40,000
Youth 20–39	Cardiology	6	477,333
	Orthopaedics	12	661,250
	Ophthalmology	1	150,000
	Cancer	7	180,000
	Kidney related	9	456,667
	Neurology	3	241,333
	Others	17	785,530
Middle-aged 40–59	Cardiology	22	355,818
	Orthopaedics	8	351,250
	Ophthalmology	1	480,000
	Cancer	33	312,697
	Kidney related	11	452,182
	Neurology	6	263,500
	Others	15	310,400
Old 60 yrs and above	Cardiology	7	320,514
	Orthopaedics	1	120,000
	Ophthalmology	1	300,000
	Cancer	3	223,333
	Kidney related	1	180,000
	Neurology	2	690,000
	Others	1	1,680,000

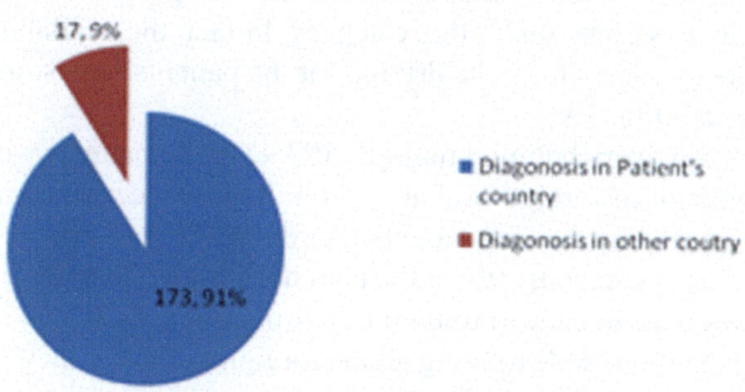

Fig. 7.5 Patients reporting diagnosis of disease

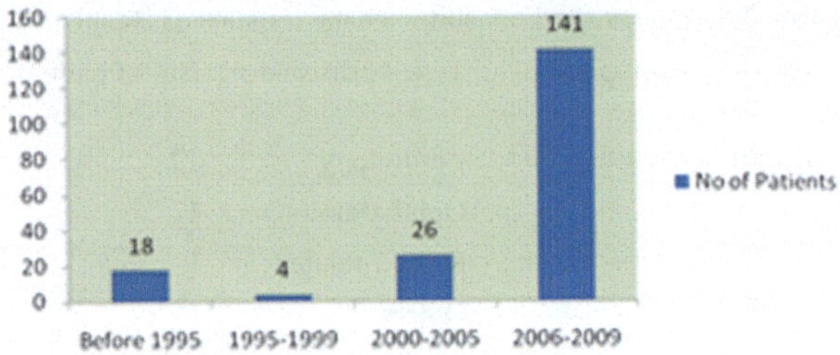

Fig. 7.6 Patients disease diagnosis distribution

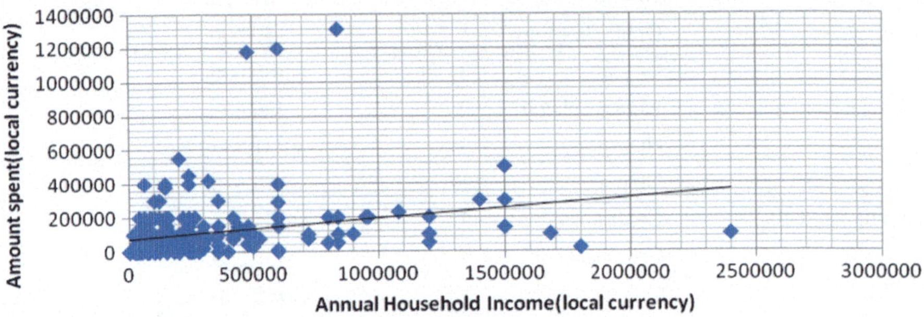

Fig. 7.7 Scatter diagram of annual household income and amount spent for medical treatment

line of best fit is quite low. This chart is only for Bangladesh patients as the amount spent is in local currency (Bangladesh Taka). The richer patients tend to spend a higher amount on an average.

Barriers and Obstacles

We now analyse the barriers to Mode 2 trade in health services in South Asia. Figure 7.8 shows that while a clear category of medical visa is available, not all patients come under this category. In fact, the availability of cheap and high quality doctors seem to be the driving for the patients' decision to visit India under "medical visa" (Fig. 7.9).

An overwhelming majority (97%) of the patients were not able to carry unlimited amount of foreign exchange from their respective country for medical treatment as reported by the respondents themselves (Fig. 7.10).

However, only 9% of the patients reported to have used the informal route to bring foreign currency to India for their treatment as shown in Fig. 7.11. Apparently, most patients are able to bring all the foreign exchange they need for the treatment through the formal route itself.

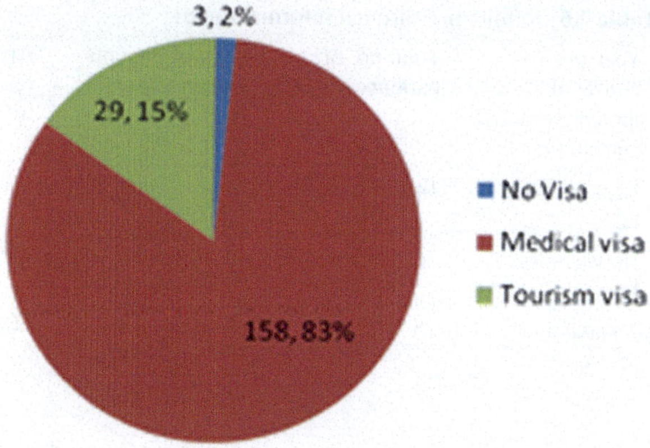

Fig. 7.8 Information barrier (visa barrier)

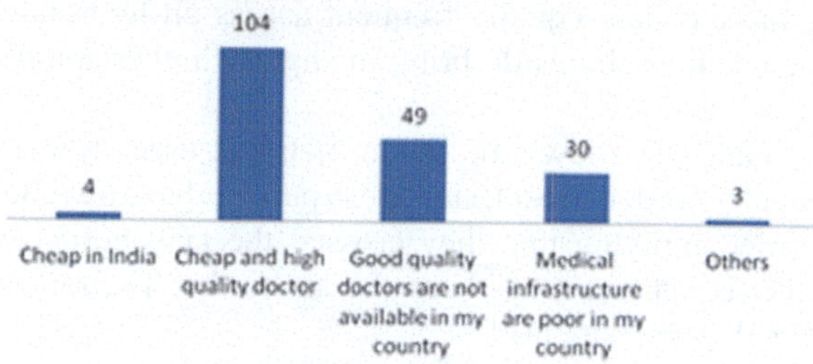

Fig. 7.9 Decision-making factors for coming to India for treatment

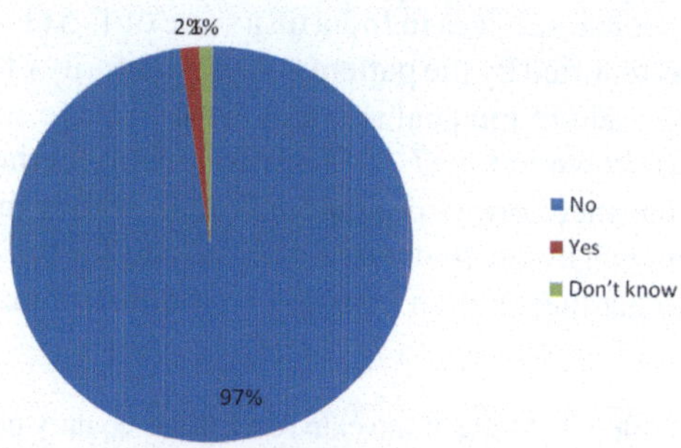

Fig. 7.10 Carrying of unlimited foreign currency

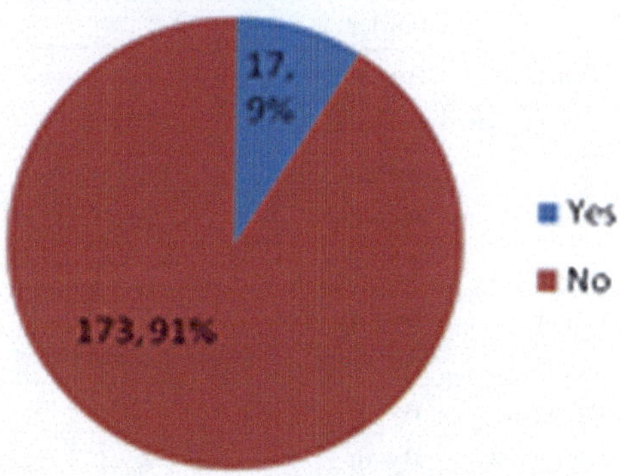

Fig. 7.11 Patients reporting remittance through informal route

Table 7.6 Remittance through informal route

Yearly household income (in local currency)	Total no. of patients	No. of patients taken informal route	Amount in remitted informally	Average Bangladesh Taka per Indian Rs. 100
Less than Rs. 5 lakh	141	11	1,100,000	145.78
Between Rs. 5 lakh and 10 lakh	26	3	485,000	146.43
10 lakh and above	15	3	600,000	147.71

Table 7.6 shows that the use of informal route for remittance of foreign exchange is more-or-less equally frequent across all household income levels. The higher-income households do bring in slightly higher amounts through the informal route on an average.

Table 7.7 shows the mode of travel used by the patients to reach their home country border. Most Bangladesh patients have travelled by road to reach their nearest border implying that they crossed the land border, while for patients from most other countries, it has been the air border. The rail route is not much preferred by Bangladeshi patients.

The next few charts assess the major obstacles to a foreign patient receiving medical services in India on a scale of 1–5 (1—minor obstacle and 5—major obstacle) as reported by the patients. A vast majority of patients feel that visa is a major obstacle to trade in medical services—the average score is 3.84 on a five-point scale of 1–5 as shown in Fig. 7.12. The bi-modality of the distribution is interesting and suggests that there are two subpopulations within the patient population. For example, for patients with contacts, it is easy, and for patients without contacts, it is very difficult to get their Indian visa and so becomes a major obstacle.

Table 7.7 Mode of travel to reach home country border

Country	Travel to nearest border	No. of patients	Total cost (in local currency)	Avg. cost (in local currency)
Afghanistan	By air	2	NA	NA
Bangladesh	By air	22	55,250	2630.95
	By rail	4	1710	427.50
	By road	156	133,565	856.19
Bhutan	By road	1	2000	2000.00
Nepal	By air	1	3500	3500.00
	By road	1	300	300.00
Pakistan	By air	1	NA	NA
Sri Lanka	By air	2	NA	NA

Fig. 7.12 Visa as an obstacle

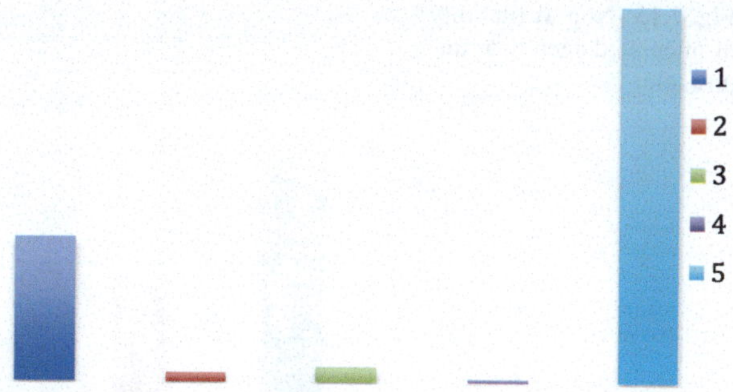

According to Fig. 7.13, the absence of right information regarding medical facilities in India and the details regarding the processes and the treatments are seen as a serious obstacle by many patients. The average score on this count works out to 1.99.

Fig. 7.13 Right information to come to India about medical facilities as an obstacle

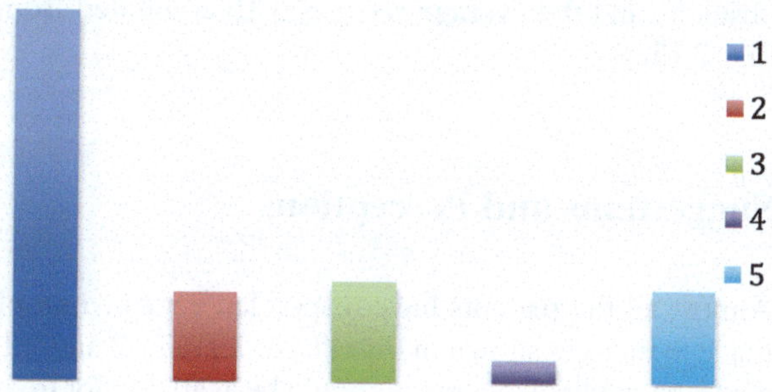

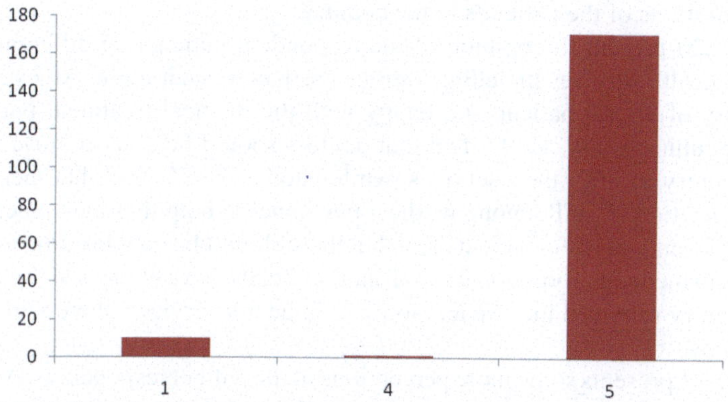

Fig. 7.14 Non-availability of Indian rail ticket as an obstacle

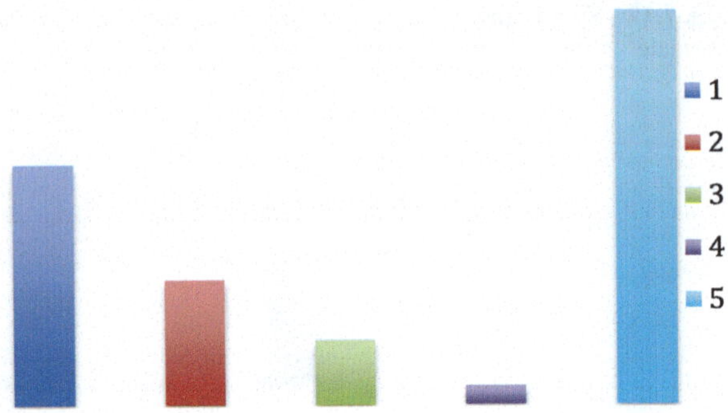

Fig. 7.15 Non-availability of integrated agency as an obstacle

Non-availability of Indian rail ticket in the patient's home country is given a score of 5 on a five-point scale by 172 patients as shown in Fig. 7.14. This raises the average score to 4.77.

An integrated agency to streamline trade in health services and handle all aspects of a foreign patient's availing of health services in India is felt lacking by many patients. In fact, many of them have felt the lack of such an integrated agency as an obstacle, and the average score is 3.10 computed from the distribution as shown in Fig. 7.15.

Suggestions and Perceptions

Almost all the patients have responded very favourably to some of the suggestions made to them as shown in Figs. 7.16, 7.17, 7.18 and 7.19. As many as 99% agree that common medical insurance should be available for treatment in any SAARC country, while 100% of them feel that hospitals should offer comprehensive packages.

Similarly, 99% of the patients feel that Indian hospitals should establish liaison outlets in their home country as well arrange to provide follow-up services in hospitals and/or institutions of the patient's home country.

Figure 7.20 present the opinion of the respondent patients on different aspects of trade in health services including various barriers to such trade. An overwhelming majority of 96.8% patients are happy with the medical treatment but feel the barriers are unnecessary. 77.9% feel that doctors should be able to move freely to another country to offer their services, while another 73.7% feel that there should be standardization of skill among medical personnel to help their movement across countries. Seventy per cent patients feel that there should be dual taxation avoidance treaty to help medical professionals, and another 76.8% have expressed the view that if their country removed the barriers to trade in health services, there will be more welfare gains.

Figure 7.21 presents some more perceptions of the patient respondents. According to 77.9% of the respondents, visa issues are complicated. About 40% patients reported

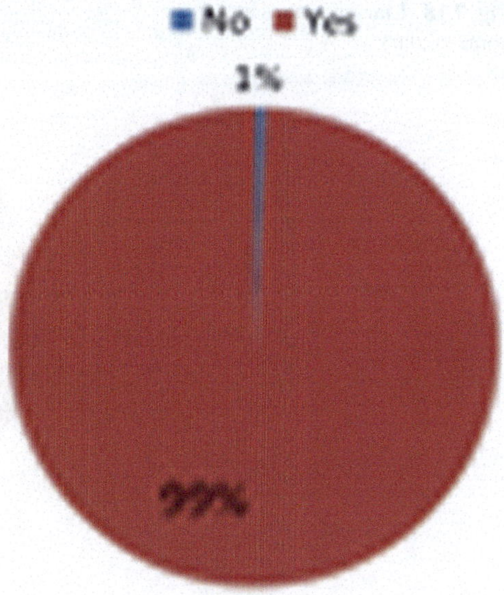

Fig. 7.16 Medical insurance for all SAARC countries

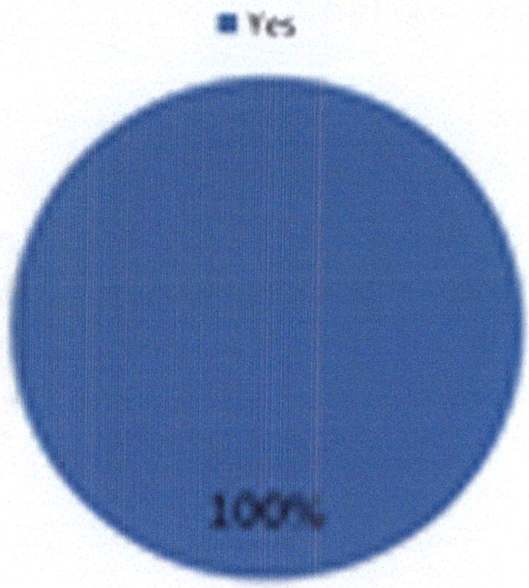

Fig. 7.17 Follow-up services in your country's hospitals/institutions

that they have been cheated by the informal foreign exchange traders, while only 19.5% reported not being cheated by them.

Fig. 7.18 Liaison outlets at home country

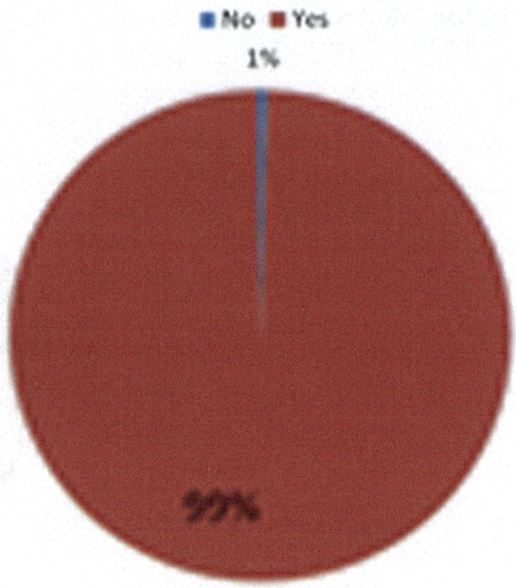

Fig. 7.19 Comprehensive package by the hospitals

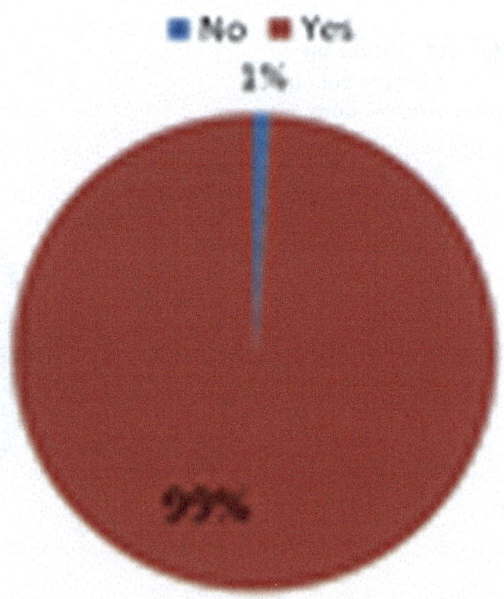

Hospitals

Table 7.8 captures different aspects of medical services offered by our sample of Indian hospitals to foreign patients. We have tabulated the information using the WTO classification of trade in services.

All the twenty hospitals surveyed reported receiving patients from some SAARC country or the other. South Indian hospitals from Bangalore and Chennai are more

	Happy with the medical treatment but the barriers are unnecessary	Current Account Convertibility	Doctors (skilled) should move freely	Standardization of skill	dual taxation treaty for medical professionals	welfare gains
Cant Say	2	139	40	48	56	41
Yes	182	46	148	140	133	146
No	6	5	2	2	1	3

Fig. 7.20 Perception 1

active in offering telemedicine services. Only six of the twenty hospitals reported that their doctors go to some neighbouring country to render professional services, and one each has stated that their doctors have gone to only Bangladesh or only Sri Lanka. Similarly, only six hospitals reported that any doctor from another SAARC country visited them over the last two years. Mode 3 services are relatively fewer and could not be captured through the questionnaires administered to the Indian hospitals.

Doctors

The questionnaire for doctors was administered to 65 doctors. The information given by doctors corroborates the information gathered from the patients that a very large

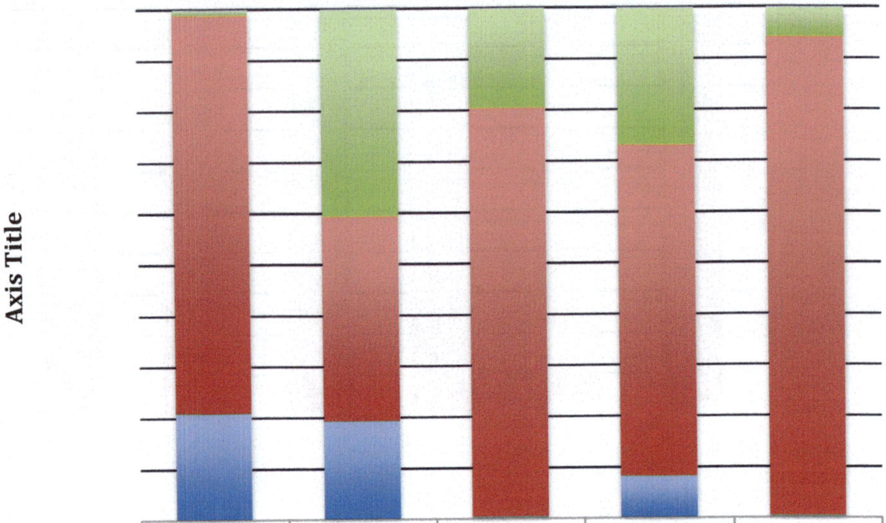

	Visa issues are complicated	Informal foreign exchange traders cheated	medical insurance policy should be applied to SAARC	Airfare is too high	access to medical services to all citizens of South Asia
Cant Say	2	77	37	51	11
Yes	148	76	152	123	178
No	40	37	1	16	1

Fig. 7.21 Perception 2

Table 7.8 Neighbouring countries visited by doctors to render medical services

Countries travelled	No. of doctors
No countries	52
Bangladesh	10
Bhutan	4
Maldives	5
Nepal	6
Pakistan	0
Sri Lanka	4
Afghanistan	0

number of the patients come from Bangladesh. In our sample, we found that Sri Lanka sent the second highest number of patients, followed by Nepal from within the SAARC. But overall, a large number of patients also come from the Gulf countries.

Out of 13 doctors that reported to have travelled to a neighbouring country to offer medical services, 10 of them reported to have travelled to Bangladesh. None of the doctors reported to have travelled to Pakistan or Afghanistan.

The doctors were asked to rate on a ten-point scale how important each of the five given possible reasons was in their decision not to move to SAARC countries. Figures 28 through 32 capture the responses of the 65 doctors.

Security environment comes out as a strong demotivating reason in Fig. 7.22. The mean score is 7.43 out of a possible 10. Figure 7.23 conveys that the attractiveness of the Indian market is reason enough for some doctors not to move to SAARC countries. The average score is 9.00.

The hassles of getting an employment permit do not appear to be a strong enough reason as the average score is 6.98 as shown in the distribution captured in Fig. 7.24. Finally, income tax policies and complications thereon are not perceived to be a

Fig. 7.22 Security environment perception

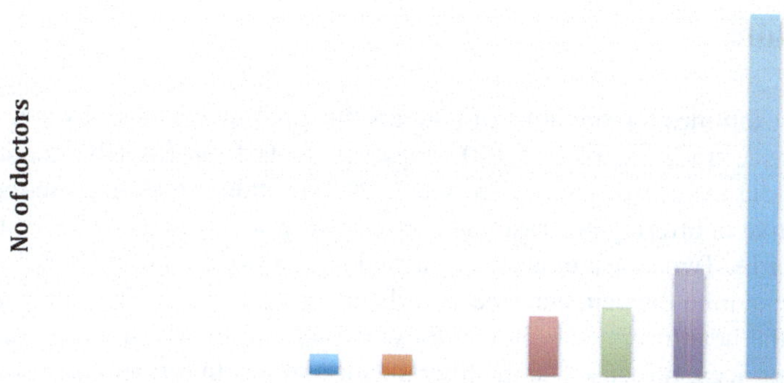

Fig. 7.23 Indian market perception

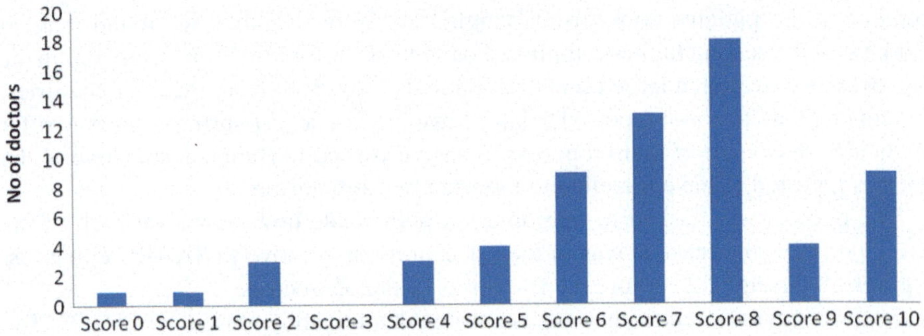

Fig. 7.24 Employment permit perception

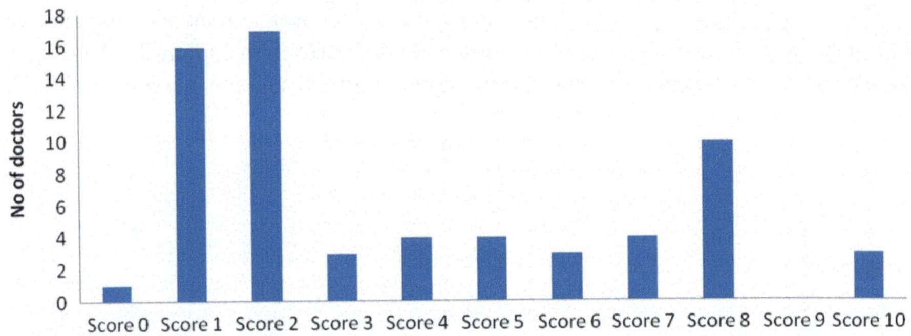

Fig. 7.25 Income tax policy perception

strong reason by the doctors. They have awarded an average score of only 3.86 to this reason (Fig. 7.25).

Conclusions

The study examines the opinions of patients, hospital owners and doctors involved in this service trade. A total of 190 foreign patients from SAARC countries that came to India to receive medical services, 20 hospitals across five metros and 65 doctors active in offering professional services were surveyed using three structured questionnaires. Two case studies were carried out on two countries (Bangladesh and Nepal) to examine the demand aspects of health service trade. This study also aims to profile the health service sector of these two countries which might affect trade in health services. It focuses on the liberalization of health services and assesses the challenges and opportunities posed by the liberalization of trade on the provisions of health services and options for national policy-makers. It further makes an effort to examine the barriers in health service trade in the two relatively small countries of South Asia. An effort is made to explore possible regional cooperation in health service trade among the above three countries of the SAARC region. The evidence is actually useful in order to understand commitments and challenges regarding trade in health services in the SAARC region.

The study opines that there exists a gender bias among the foreign patients coming to India for medical treatment. An overwhelming majority (about 79.5%) of the patients is male, and more than half are in the age group of 40–59. Not so surprisingly, about 95.8% of the patients are from Bangladesh. The largest number of patients (46%) is self-employed followed by another 30% in private service. About 12% of the patient's sources of income are agriculture. Surprisingly, about 10% of the patients are in government service in their respective country which implies a perceived lack of medical facilities even for government servants.

The largest number of patients coming to India is for cardiac (49) and cancer (45) treatment. Orthopaedic (21) and kidney-related (22) treatment also forms a significant percentage. A little bi-modality among cardiology patients—both juvenile (under 19) and middle-aged patients outnumber youth in the sample—is noticed by the study. The dominance of males across all age groups and across all disease categories is also clearly visible—the only exception being patients who are between 20 and 39 years old and do not have any of the stated diseases. This may be due to gynaecological problems that are faced by the female youth patients.

Majority of the patients get their diagnosis done in their home country. Apparently, the local doctors advise them to go abroad for better treatment in view of insufficient facilities and expertise in the home country. In many cases, the issue of travelling to India for treatment comes after several months of diagnosis.

As many as 15% of the patients were found to have entered India on tourist visa implying that the higher transaction cost of getting a medical visa is much more than the higher perceived value for the same. Over 85% of the patients have entered India on a one-month single-entry visa. The related uncertainty and anxiety would be adding to the cost associated with the patient's treatment in India. About 11% of the patients admitted to using the services of a broker or a middleman for their visa.

A vast majority (104 out of 190) of patients reported that they came to India because of its inexpensive and high-quality doctors—a pull factor—while 49 and 30 reported the absence of good-quality doctors and medical infrastructure, respectively, in their home country—a distinctive push factor. Regarding remittance of foreign exchange, the higher-income households do bring in slightly higher amounts through the informal route. There is no particular relationship between the rates at which Indian rupee is bought by the Bangladesh patients and their respective household income.

This study also studied the major obstacles to a foreign patient receiving medical services in India on a scale of 1–5. It turns out that visa is a major obstacle to trade in medical services (average score 3.84). However, non-availability of Indian rail ticket in the patient's home country is given a score of 5 on a five-point scale by 172 patients. This raises the average score to 4.77. An integrated agency to streamline trade in health services and handle all aspects of a foreign patient's availing of health services in India is felt lacking by many patients. In fact, many of them have felt the lack of such an integrated agency as an obstacle.

An overwhelming majority of patients (96.8%) are happy with the medical treatment but feel that the barriers in this respect are unnecessary. Surprisingly, as many as 73.2% have no particular view on current account convertibility, and only 24.2% feel that their country should have it. Between 70 and 80% patients feel that doctors should be able to move freely to another country, that there should be standardization of skill among medical personnel, that there should be dual taxation treaty to help medical professionals and that if their country removed the barriers to trade in health services, there will be more welfare gains. According to 77.9% of the respondents, visa issues are complicated. About 40% patients reported that they have been cheated by the informal foreign exchange traders, while only 19.5% reported not being cheated by them. A clear eighty per cent of the patients have opined that their medical insurance policy should be valid across all SAARC countries and another 64.7% patients feel that the airfare is too high.

All twenty hospitals surveyed reported receiving patients from some SAARC country or the other. South Indian hospitals from Bangalore and Chennai are more active in offering telemedicine services. Only six hospitals reported that any doctor from another SAARC country visited them over the last two years. As expected, none of the hospitals are having any Mode 3 medical service.

Doctors corroborate the information gathered from the patients that a very large number of the patients come from Bangladesh. In our sample, we found that Sri Lanka sent the second highest number of patients, followed by Nepal from within the SAARC. But overall, a large number of patients also come from the Gulf countries. Only 20% of the doctors surveyed travel to SAARC countries to treat patients. This percentage is still fairly high considering that Mode 4 service trade is perhaps the most restrictive among all the four modes.

Security environment comes out as a strong demotivating reason discouraging movement of doctors. The attractiveness of the Indian market is reason enough for some doctors not to move to SAARC countries. The hassles of getting an employment permit, complicated visa process or income tax policies and complications thereon also do not appear to be strong enough reasons. In summary, Mode 4 service seems to have the highest potential to offer the maximum welfare gain in South Asia.

The case study on Bangladesh reveals the fact that telemedicine services may help Bangladesh to provide better services to its people, side by side checking illegal money transfer to neighbouring countries. Telemedicine may assist more consumers to get access to faster, better and possibly cheaper diagnostic medical services, including some therapeutic services. It should be borne in mind that there may be weak consumer protection, and for this reason, additional inter-country agreements are needed.

It is understood that telemedicine and teleconferencing services between the SAARC countries can help to import and export services and accordingly benefit and improve the services of both private and public hospitals of the SAARC region. Currently, Bhutan and India have already entered into the network and are reaping the benefit of this technology; unfortunately, the Bangladesh government has not taken any effective initiative in this respect, and the country still remains outside the SAARC telemedicine network. Countries like Bangladesh, Nepal and Afghanistan, for example, can join in the regional group like SAARC telemedicine network and provide its citizens faster, superior and cheaper diagnostic medical services, including some therapeutic services through regional telemedicine services.

It is observed that Mode 2 provides quality treatment to Bangladeshi patients and there is little doubt that a huge amount of foreign exchange of Bangladesh outflows to foreign countries, often through illegal channel as Bangladeshi patients spend huge amount of foreign exchange in India and East Asian countries like Thailand and Singapore for receiving treatments.

The study opines that commercial presence in health services (Mode 3) can create supplementary resources for investment in and upgrading of healthcare infrastructure and technologies of the country. The availability of private capital in the country may reduce the total burden on government resources and may help to generate employment. Inflow of foreign capital in certain parts of the health system (e.g. establishment of hospitals with modern facilities) may reduce the burden on government resources and allow the public sector to relocate its resources towards the patients with less ability to pay. The presence of foreign commercial firms (with higher levels of pay and/or better equipment and premises) may entice Bangladesh health personnel away from public facilities: an 'internal' brain drain. For this reason, there is a need to formulate effective public policy to check it, and there is a need to impose limitations on FDI in health services.

There are also other possible negative effects of FDI in health services in Bangladesh, e.g. excessive technological dependence, capital flight and profit outflow. All these may lead to negative effects on the Bangladesh's balance of payments. It may also make foreign medical services affordable to wealthy persons and to those with expensive medical insurance. It is generally observed that foreign private health service providers try to offer services which are not offered by the public sector. These services are usually given to attract affluent customers.

The study further observes that FDI actually enhances commercialization of the healthcare sector of Bangladesh. Bangladesh, therefore, should take a step back and deeply study the above issues of the risk and benefits of commercialization of its health sector and then decide whether this sector should be opened up to foreign investment or not.

It is noted that temporary movement of personnel (Mode 4) may assist Bangladesh and other SAARC countries to receive essential healthcare services. It is felt that Bangladesh would be benefited substantially through increased export of service providers (e.g. doctor and nurses) through TMNP. It has been noticed that there exist severe disparities in the number of health personnel among SAARC countries. TMNP may make health services more accessible and affordable, thus increasing the welfare of the SAARC countries. In this respect, some constructive knowledge spillover effects are also possible. TMNP can assist to reduce these disparities and help to reduce the shortages of health professionals. Bhutan has already shown interest to employ Bangladeshi doctors in the hospitals of country. This is a significant signal for Bangladesh indeed. Bangladesh can adopt an effective domestic health policy in this respect. For opening up market in the SAARC region and also in the developed countries, Bangladesh government should identify current capacity of supply of health professionals within the country.

Special type of visa may be introduced for the SAARC countries in this respect. Indian proposal on GATS visa is gradually becoming popular in both developed members and developing members who successfully distinguished between temporary provision of service supply and migration (Bhattacharya et al. 2003). Some developing countries, e.g. Tunisia, earn huge amount of foreign exchange through health service trading. Tunisia has probably the highest potential for health services exports in the Middle East and North Africa (MENA) region (Lautier 2008), and a country like Bangladesh can follow the model of Tunisia in this respect.

Bangladesh government should also devise a long-term plan for health service trade. Identification of market and negotiations for market access should be linked with health professional's skill development plan. The number one priority in upcoming negotiations for Bangladesh in health service trade should be TMNP under Mode 4. The liberalization of health sector with limited opening of Mode 4 in the SAARC region will bring positive result in reducing deficit in trade in health services, improving quality of health services and enhancing technology transfer. The policy of exporting health service providers through TMNP requires plans for attraction of returned migrants, an essential element of which is to help them to be effectively absorbed into the domestic labour market (Raihan and Mahmood 2004). It is also understood that in designing health service trade in future under SAFTA, it is vital to protect the interests of the smaller and weaker economies of the SAARC regions, e.g. Bangladesh, Sri Lanka, Nepal, Maldives and Afghanistan, so that these countries can constructively engage themselves in benefiting from access to a free trade area.

Chapter 8
Summary and Conclusions

Arindam Banik

Healthcare policymakers in South Asia struggle with the conflicting goals of providing ready access to medical care with rising costs. The challenges are particularly acute where outcomes are uncertain, and there exists poor quality of treatment in the respective countries due to underdeveloped health infrastructure. To investigate the impact of these, this study is aimed at understanding the structure of health services and their assessments. The study has also evaluated the economic costs of barriers to trade in health services in select South Asian economies such as Bangladesh, India, Pakistan, Sri Lanka and Nepal based on primary survey.

We first portray the scenario of health care in India in the light of the possible implementation of universal health coverage (UHC). The analysis reveals that the existing schemes have not succeeded in achieving the desired objectives and targets. This unveils interesting insights—one, private financial insurance fails to provide financial protection, and two, public financial protection arrangements are weak. We find that government allocation on health out of total government expenditure has not risen over the years and private health expenditure and voluntary health insurance are the dominant source of health spending and financing. However, such expenditures are now slowly picking up but they are grossly inadequate. Another facet of our findings is inadequate nature of publicly provided healthcare facilities and privately provided facilities that are not affordable.

[1] Anganwadi is a type of rural child care centre in India. They were started by the Indian government in 1975 as part of the Integrated Child Development Services programme to combat child hunger and malnutrition. Anganwadi means "courtyard shelter" in Indian languages.

The author would like to express their deepest gratitude to the South Asia Network for Economic Institutionbs (SANEI) in Kathmandu, Nepal for allowing us to use some contents of the Chapter 8 of the report entitled,"Trade in Health Services in South Asia: An Examination of the Need for Regional Cooperation", submitted by the authors in 2008.

A. Banik (✉)
International Management Institute, Kolkata, India

A. Banik (ed.), *Trade in Health Services in South Asia*,
https://doi.org/10.1007/978-981-15-2191-1_8

India may also think of providing primary health care for all and creating 'community health workers' by providing basic medical training and small incentive to *Anganwadi*[1] workers to take care of basic health care for all in publicly provided primary healthcare centres where services are free of cost. Gradually, the coverage may be extended to more complex healthcare services. This might be a step forward to achieve desirable health outcomes as well as reduce the incidence of catastrophic expenditure and impoverishment over time. Moreover, this will not involve extra financial burden on the government, but may ensure basic health care for all. Since such community health workers operate at the local level, creation of awareness about general health, diseases as well as prevention of certain diseases will also be possible. Developing countries have proved that low income and comprehensive health care are not mutually exclusive. Hence in India, instead of relying on publicly financed health insurance schemes and high-cost privately provided healthcare services, policymakers should focus on more efficient use of government funds through targeting universal basic health care in achieving the objective of access to health care and financial protection for all.

Healthcare systems in India's neighbourhood are equally inadequate and inefficient. Countries belonging to South Asian region have already liberalized their services sectors to a certain extent through unilateral, multilateral and regional initiatives. Under the GATS, most South Asian countries (other than Bhutan) have made commitments.

The case study on Bangladesh reveals the fact that telemedicine services may help Bangladesh to provide better services to its people and simultaneously check illegal money transfer to neighbouring countries. Telemedicine may assist more consumers to get access to faster, better and possibly cheaper diagnostic medical services, including some therapeutic services. It should be borne in mind that there may be weak consumer protection and so additional inter-country agreements are needed.

It is understood that telemedicine and teleconferencing services between the SAARC countries can help to import and export services and accordingly benefit and improve the services of both private and public hospitals of the SAARC region. Currently, Bhutan and India have already entered into the network and are reaping the benefit of this technology. However, Bangladesh government has not taken any effective initiative in this respect and the country still remains outside the SAARC Telemedicine Network. Countries like Bangladesh, Nepal and Afghanistan, for example, can join in the regional group like SAARC Telemedicine Network and provide its citizens faster, superior and cheaper diagnostic medical services, including some therapeutic services through regional telemedicine services.

It is observed that Mode 2 provides quality treatment to Bangladeshi patients and there is little doubt that a huge outflow of foreign exchange from Bangladesh to foreign countries occurs, often through illegal channel as Bangladeshi patients spend huge amount of foreign exchange in India and East Asian countries like Thailand and Singapore for receiving treatments.

The study opines that commercial presence in health services (Mode 3) can create supplementary resources for investment in and upgrading of healthcare infrastructure and technologies of the country. The availability of private capital in the country may reduce the total burden on government resources and may help to generate employment. Inflow of foreign capital in certain parts of the health system (e.g. establishment of hospitals with modern facilities) may reduce the burden on government resources and allow the public sector to relocate its resources towards the patients with less ability to pay. The presence of foreign commercial firms (with higher levels of pay and/or better equipment and premises) may entice Bangladesh health personnel away from public facilities: an 'internal' brain drain. For this reason, there is a need to formulate effective public policy to check it and there is a need to impose limitations on FDI in health services.

There are also other possible negative effects of FDI in health services in Bangladesh, e.g. excessive technological dependence, capital flight and profit outflow. All these may lead to negative effects on Bangladesh's balance of payments. It may also make foreign medical services affordable to wealthy persons and to those with expensive medical insurance. It is generally observed that foreign private health service providers try to offer services which are not offered by the public sector. These services are usually given to attract affluent customers.

The study further observes that FDI actually enhances commercialization of the healthcare sector of Bangladesh. Bangladesh, therefore, should take a step back, deeply study the above issues of the risk and benefits of commercialization of its health sector and then decide whether this sector should be opened up to foreign investment or not.

It is noted that temporary movement of personnel (Mode 4) may assist Bangladesh and other SAARC countries to receive essential healthcare services. It is felt that Bangladesh would be benefited substantially through increased export of service providers (e.g. doctor and nurses) through TMNP. It has been noticed that there exist severe disparities in the number of health personnel among SAARC countries. TMNP may make health services more accessible and affordable, thus increasing the welfare of the SAARC countries. In this respect, some constructive knowledge spillover effects are also possible. TMNP can assist to reduce these disparities and help to reduce the shortages of health professionals. Bhutan has already shown interest to employ Bangladeshi doctors in the hospitals of country. This is a significant signal for Bangladesh indeed. Bangladesh can adopt an effective domestic health policy in this respect. For opening up market in the SAARC region and also in the developed countries, Bangladesh government should identify current capacity of supply of health professionals within the country.

Special type of visa may be introduced for the SAARC countries in this respect. Indian proposal on GATS visa is gradually becoming popular in both developed country members and developing country members who successfully distinguished between temporary provision of service supply and migration (Bhattacharya et al. 2003). Some developing countries, e.g. Tunisia, earn huge amount of foreign exchange through health service trading. Tunisia has probably the highest potential for health services exports in the Middle East and North Africa (MENA) region (Lautier 2008), and a country like Bangladesh can follow the model of Tunisia in this respect.

The study reveals that historically in the South Asian region Sri Lanka has been recognized as one of the best performers in the health sector. Sri Lanka for its efficient health policies could achieve the Millennium Development Goals (MDGs) set by the United Nations much ahead of its target time and quite effectively, specially in the domain of communicable diseases, as compared to many other low–middle-income countries in the region. However, Sri Lanka is undergoing massive epidemiological transition in the recent times with more observed NCD cases rather than communicable diseases—which has so far been the thrust area of health policies and public health financing in the country. Likewise, old age population is on the rise, implying changes in the expected disease pattern in the near future. Therefore, health policy preparedness is urgently needed in order to accommodate this massive demographic transition. Sri Lanka has been quite well known for its cheap health services in the South Asian region; however, concerns over access to quality health services and equity in such services have been the focal points of policy discussions. While Sri Lanka could plan suitably for the UHC component of widening service delivery given its wide health service coverage that was already prevailing in the public health system, Sri Lanka is yet to design credible and effective policies towards the dimension of catastrophic health financing component to meet the set targets of UHC under SDG. Lastly, the healthcare dependency of the patients in the secondary and tertiary health care rather than the primary health care has been an outcome of an intrinsically erroneous incentive designing mechanism in Sri Lanka's public health system. This needs to be addressed urgently.

The study unveils that the current healthcare spending in Pakistan is abysmally low as compared to many other low–middle-income peers, about USD 17 per capita with government's contribution being only a quarter. On the other hand, health outcomes are also not satisfactory, and far below the WHO recommended benchmarks. In terms of health outcome indicators like IMR, MMR and life expectancy at birth, Pakistan is lagging behind; although visible improvements are happening with respect to MMR and LEB, negligible decline in the infant mortality rate is a growing cause of concern. In this chapter, we have built an experimental health outcome index. According to the index, Pakistan is far away from other emerging countries in the region. This signals cost effective interventions in the health sector in Pakistan should be prioritized, especially related to pre-natal and post-natal care, increasing the percentage of births attended by skilled health staff, increasing immunization coverage, and improving access to clean water and good quality sanitation and nutritional outcomes. In recent times, in order to meet the SDGs several innovative health financing steps have been taken by the private sector, NGOs and the government of Pakistan, specially towards UHC and social protection. The chapter also discusses the new health financing mechanisms such as Heartfile Health Financing (HHF) which are being implemented in phased manner in Pakistan as pilot projects and are recognized widely to be commendable steps towards mobilizing resources and increasing efficiency in health sector financing. If such pilots are found to be successful, these mechanisms can be replicated for other low–middle-income countries as well.

The study on Nepal healthcare system observed that health services at most of the public institutions in Nepal are subsidized by the government and services are generally provided from public good perspective. This implies that such public institutions are less important from the trade viewpoint. Therefore, greater involvement of the private sector particularly in operating teaching hospitals and tertiary care, and liberalization of the policies for exporting health services are necessary for exporting the services.

The study finds that the most of the patients arrived in Nepal from India belong to low-income households. However, some patients have expressed their willingness to pay even higher fees for the services if they were referring to arrange additional and fringe benefits while consuming the health services. Therefore, provision of at least two or three levels of fee structure with differing facilities particularly at specialty and high-cost treatment providers should be arranged to attract high-income foreign people for service consumption. Rather than the general services, Indian patients are found to be interested in the specialty and chronic problem-related services. Therefore, Indian patient-targeted departments with relevant services should be established particularly in the hospitals which are nearer to India. In doing so, priority should be given to the illness requiring high-cost treatment so that volume of the trade would be large. The study emphasizes that effective information channel needs to be developed to attract larger flow of the patients from the foreign land. Many patients are facing problems in identifying appropriate service provider because of the non-availability of the information regarding available services and the cost structure in different institutions.

It seems useful to mention here that a different stratum of patients can be attracted in Nepalese hospitals if some unique features can be incorporated in the domestic service system. For this purpose, more focus should be given on research activities for exploring the locally available natural resources that are useful in the treatment and at the same time for developing country-specific unique method of treatment and promoting traditional methods of treatment. Quality of the services is one of the most important elements to attract patients in a particular health institution. Therefore, Nepal government should make necessary provisions for assuring quality of the health services.

Some of the advanced countries such as USA and Canada have high demand for low-cost health service providers, particularly from developing countries. To fulfil this gap in those countries and for the promotion of service export through the bilateral agreements, efforts should be made to attract FDI to raise the production of human resources in the domestic country. By this means, export of health service can be facilitated mainly via Mode 4.

Despite the increasing inflow of non-Indian tourists, health tourism is found virtually limited to Indian service consumers in Nepal. Therefore, there is need to integrate health services with the tourism for exporting services to non-Indian foreigners via second mode. For this purpose, gradually tourists can be attracted for the treatment purpose in the country by making them familiar with the domestic service system through the arrangement of health services in the tour package, etc.

Management tie-up and the expansion of the network of the domestic service providers with the reputed foreign health service providers and insurance companies are important for exporting services via both second and third modes. The Nepalese government can encourage this primarily through policy adjustments. In the present context of increasing role played by the private sector, the purpose of regulating the health services in the country and registering medical practitioners according to their qualifications by establishing a medical council as provisioned in Nepal Medical Council Act seems relevant. Initiation should be taken in this line to ensure quality services and bring homogeneity in the services which are important elements to attract foreign patients for service consumption.

In order to gain insights into the trade in health services in India, the study examines the opinions of patients, hospital owners and doctors involved in this service trade. A total of 190 foreign patients from Bangladesh, Nepal, Sri Lanka and Afghanistan who came to India to receive medical services, 20 hospitals across five metros and 65 doctors active in offering professional services were surveyed using three structured questionnaires. It focuses on the liberalization of health services and assesses the challenges and opportunities posed by the liberalization of trade on the provisions of health services and options for national policymakers. It further makes an effort to examine the barriers in health service trade in the two relatively small countries of South Asia. An effort is made to explore possible regional cooperation in health service trade among the above three countries of the SAARC region. The evidence is actually useful in order to understand commitments and challenges regarding trade in health services in the SAARC region.

The study finds that there exists a gender bias among the foreign patients coming to India for medical treatment. The largest number of patients (46%) is self-employed followed by another 30% in private service. About 12% of the patient's sources of income are agriculture. Surprisingly, about 10% of the patients are in government service in their respective country which implies a perceived lack of medical facilities even for government servants.

The largest number of patients coming to India is for cardiac (49) and cancer (45) treatment. Orthopaedic (21) and kidney-related (22) treatments also form a significant percentage. A little bi-modality among cardiology patients—both juvenile (under 19) and middle-aged patients outnumber youth in the sample—is noticed by the study. The dominance of males across all age groups and across all disease categories is also clearly visible—the only exception being patients who are between 20 and 39 years old and do not have any of the stated diseases. This may be due to gynaecological problems that are faced by the female youth patients.

We observe that a vast majority (104 out of 190) of patients reported that they came to India because of its inexpensive and high-quality doctors—a pull factor—while 49 and 30 reported the absence of good-quality doctors and medical infrastructure, respectively, in their home country—a distinctive push factor. Regarding remittance of foreign exchange, the higher-income households do bring in slightly higher amounts through the informal route. The study opines that an integrated agency to streamline trade in health services and handle all aspects of a foreign patients availing of health services in India is felt lacking by many patients. In fact, many of them have felt the lack of such an integrated agency as an obstacle.

An overwhelming majority of patients (96.8%) are happy with the medical treatment but feel that the barriers in this respect are unnecessary. Between 70 and 80%

patients feel that doctors should be able to move freely to another country, there should be standardization of skill among medical personnel, there should be dual taxation treaty to help medical professionals and if their country removed the barriers to trade in health services, there will be more welfare gains.

All twenty hospitals surveyed reported receiving patients from one SAARC country or the other. South Indian hospitals from Bangalore and Chennai are more active in offering telemedicine services. Only six hospitals reported that any doctor from another SAARC country visited them over the last two years. As expected, none of the hospitals are having any Mode 3 medical service.

Doctors corroborate the information gathered from the patients that a very large number of the patients come from Bangladesh. In our sample, we found that Sri Lanka sent the second highest number of patients, followed by Nepal from within the SAARC. But overall, a large number of patients also come from the gulf countries. Only, 20% of the doctors surveyed travel to SAARC countries to treat patients. This percentage is still fairly high considering that Mode 4 services trade is perhaps the most restrictive among all the four modes.

Security comes out as a strong demotivating reason discouraging movement of doctors. The attractiveness of the Indian market is a reason enough for some doctors not to move to SAARC countries. The hassles of getting an employment permit, complicated visa process or income tax policies and complications thereon also do not appear to be strong enough reasons. On the whole analysis, Mode 4 service seems to have the highest potential to offer the maximum welfare gain in South Asia.

This study has put forward some policy implications. The findings of the study suggest that there exists a huge arbitrage opportunity for the local professionals and other local service providers in a particular economy due to demand and supply gap. To achieve greater economic welfare, the barriers have to be removed, defined by modes 3 and 4. The organization of a regional skills council for standardization of skills would be very important to take advantage of the arbitrage opportunity. Once these are identified, then investments may be encouraged and in the process movement of natural persons without barriers such as simplified visa, favourable work permit, dual taxation, among others, may be resolved. This is a kind of win-win situation in the light of economic welfare gains in the region.

The study has four strong policy implications for services trade sector in South Asia. First, due to abundance of trained and skilled professionals in health services India has advantage in cross-border supply (i.e. in modes 1 and 2) Therefore, opening up of cross-border supply of services in these sectors would strengthen services trade flows through modes 1 and 2 in the region. The member countries and their highly skilled population can also be benefited with the help of an integrated region. Second, with regard to trade in services under Mode 3 (commercial presence), South Asian countries should further liberalize FDI and adopt transparent domestic regulations in the areas of health services. Besides, domestic reforms and liberalization would lead to generate higher FDI under Mode 3 in the region. Third, SAARC region is one of the most important exporters of services through the movement of natural persons (Mode 4). Bangladesh, India, Pakistan and Sri Lanka have large endowments of labour at all skill levels and have a comparative advantage in exporting services through this mode of supply. South Asian countries should therefore expect liberalization of movement of natural persons for professional services from developed and other developing countries. Fourth, many have argued that the level of education is below the performance required to integrate entrants to the labour force. The modes are important implications for understanding technology spillover in health sector across South Asian economies.

What emerges is that South Asian countries have to take cautious but forward-looking steps in order to remove the trade restrictions in services trade in general and health sector in particular. These are the sectors which drive services trade in many of the South Asian countries and also provide employment. Therefore, adequate reforms may not only remove the barriers to services trade but also generate higher services trade in the region, through which the region may achieve higher income and employment. This will ultimately strengthen the overall services trade capacity of the region, which is remarkably skewed at present.

Trade liberalization, under multilateral broad-based negotiations, is important because it provides an opportunity for the countries to gain visible benefits for their exporters from opening up of markets. The WTO has proven a powerful means for countries to promote economic growth and development resulting in creation of new jobs and narrowing the development gaps. This study envisages that SAARC as a regional trading bloc can also promote growth, generate employment and strengthen overall development of the region.

As a next step, an assessment of the impact of the different reforms engaged by the sample countries would be useful. However, such an evaluation is not an easy task given the multiplicity of direct and indirect effects. Ex ante and ex post qualitative and quantitative assessments must be conducted at the sectoral level but also at the economy-wide level to capture the interaction between the various sectoral reforms and the impact on other sectors.

The world as we know today will undergo major changes by the middle of this century. The countries that are unable or slow to respond will have to make room for others that can move quicker, and innovation will be the key differentiating factor. In the long term, it may even be possible for some economies to survive only on the basis of their capital or technology, but labour alone may be unable to provide this sustenance. By bringing a large part of their population to the economic marketplace, the South Asian nations may set free their innovation potential which has so far not found any route to reach the market. When this happens, the region will surely be a different place with many possibilities.

References

Alam SMI (1986) Job satisfaction: a case study of working women in different garment factories in Dhaka City. J Manage Bus Econ 12(1):72–88

Andaleeb SS (2006) Choice and evaluation of hospitals in Bangladesh: insights from patients and poly implications. J Health Population Dev Countries 1(2):19–28

Andaleeb SS (2007) Patient satisfaction with health services in Bangladesh. Health Policy Plan 22:263–273

Bajracharya BB, Bajracharya R (2008), Endline evaluation of the community based trafficking prevention initiatives project. Submitted to save the children. Technical Review Group Pvt. Ltd., Kathmandu

Bangladesh Bank, Bangladesh Bank Enterprise Survey, various issues

Banik A, De P, Bhaumik PK (2009) Measuring the Barriers to trade in services in South Asia: an empirical exercise. International Management Institute, Mimeo

Banik A, Bhaumik PK, Monzurul Huq SM, Bajracharya BB (2014) Trade in health services in South Asia: an examination of the need for regional cooperation. In: Mujeri MF, Mahmud W (eds) Adjusting to global economic volatality: the case of South Asia. Academic Foundation, New Delhi, pp 285–360

Barai-Jaitly T, Ghosh S (2018) Role of government in funded health insurance schemes. Econ Polit Weekly LIII(25):21–23

Belsky L, Lie R, Mattoo A (2004) The general agreement in trade in services: implications for health policymakers. Health Affairs 23(3):137–145

Bhattacharya D (2002) Foreign direct investment in South Asia: promises and pitfalls. In: Presented the paper for the roundtable on "Government-Industry Partnership: Sourcing Foreign Direct Investment for Poverty Alleviation in SAARC Countries" held in Paradise Island, Maldives, 29 September–1 October 2002

Bhattacharya D (2005) Least developed countries in trade negotiations: planning process and information needs. In: Paper 52. Centre for Policy Dialogue, Dhaka, Bangladesh

Bhattacharyay B (2007) Deepening India–Bangladesh economic cooperation: challenges and opportunities. In: Discussion paper #130. Research and Information System for Developing Countries (RIS), New Delhi

Bhattacharya D, Rahman M, Raihan A, Tipu MA, Khatun FA (2003) Ongoing WTO negotiations and Bangladesh's interests: insights from CPD's October 2002 tracking mission to Geneva. In: CPD occasional paper 34. Centre for Policy Dialogue, Dhaka

Blouin C (2006) International trade in health services and the GATS. In: Presentation at the CEEC, La Havana, July 13–14

Broens THF (2007) Determinants of successful telemedicine implementations: a literature study. J Telemed Telecare 13:303–309

A. Banik (ed.), *Trade in Health Services in South Asia*,
https://doi.org/10.1007/978-981-15-2191-1

Cartwright L (2000) Reach out and heal someone: Rural telemedicine and the globalization of US health care. In: Brodwin P (ed) Biotechnology and culture, bodies, anxieties, ethic. Indiana University Press, Bloomington

Chanda R (2001) Movement of natural persons and the GATS. Report written for the Indian Council for Research on International Economic Relations, New Delhi, India (Excerpt published by Blackwell Publishers, Oxford, UK)

Chanda R (2002) Trade in health services. Indian Council for Research on International Economic Relations, Mimeo, New Delhi

Chanda R (2003) Social services and the GATS: key issues and concerns. World Dev 31(12):1997–2011

Chia NC, Whalley J (1997) A numerical example showing globally welfare-worsening liberalization of international trade in banking services. J Policy Model 19(2):119–127

Cotlear D, Smith O (2015) How 24 developing countries are implementing universal health coverage reforms from the bottom up. International Bank for Reconstruction and Development/The World Bank, Going Universal, 99455

Dacanay JC, Rodolfo MCL (2005) Challenges in health services trade: Philippines case. In: Discussion paper series no. 2005–30. Philippines Institute for Development Studies, Philippines

Dieleman JL et al (2017) Future and potential spending on health 2015–40: Development assistance for health, and government, prepaid private, and out-of pocket health spending in 184 countries. Lancet 389:2005–2030

Dixit H (2004) Health in quest. Kathmandu, Nepal

Findlay C, Warren T (2000) Introduction. In: Findlay C, Warren T (eds) Impediments to trade in services: measurement and policy implications. Routledge, London, pp 1–20

Ghosh S (2018) Publicly financed health insurance schemes. Econ Polit Weekly LIII(23):16–18

Government of Bangladesh (2001) Bangladesh Health Bulletin, various issues. Directorate General of Health Services (DGHS), Dhaka

Handicap. International (2008) Situation of physically disable in Central Terai of Nepal. Kathmandu

Hjelm NM (2005) Benefits and drawbacks of telemedicine. J Telemed Telecare 11:60–70

Hjortsberg CA, Mwikisa CN (2002) Cost of access to health services in Zambia. Health Policy Plan 17(1):71–77

Hooda SK (2017) Health payments and household well-being—how effective are heath policy interventions? Econ Polit Weekly LII(16):54–65

Huque SMR (2000) Consumers' perception on health service marketing of private hospitals in Dhaka Metropolitan Area. Unpublished Masters' thesis. Department of Business Administration, Jahangirnagar University, Savar, Dhaka, Bangladesh

IHE (2002) Cross border health care: a study of determinants for patients in Kolkata from Bangladesh. Institute of Health Economics, University of Dhaka, Dhaka

Karan A et al (2017) Extending health insurance to the poor in India: An impact evaluation of Rashtriya Swasthya Bima Yojana on out of pocket spending for healthcare. Soc Sci Med 181:83–92

Keane MP, Thakur R (2018), Health care spending and hidden poverty in India. In: UNSW business school research paper no. 2018 ECON 02, UNSW Business School, Australia

Kelegama S (2009) Trade in services in South Asia. SAGE, India

Kelegama S, Mukherjee IN (2007) India–Sri Lanka bilateral free trade agreement: six years performance and beyond. In: RIS discussion paper #119, New Delhi

Khor M (2006) UNCTAD panel debates state of WTO services negotiations, Geneva, 10 Feb 2006.

Lautier M (2008) Export of health services from developing countries: the case of Tunesia. Social Science and Medicine 67(1):101–110

Madurawela S (2016) Health care financing in Sri Lanka: challenges and alternatives. Srilanka state of the economy report, Chapter 8

Maskay NM (2006) Foreign investment liberalization and incentives in selected Asia-Pacific developing countries: implications for the health service sector in Nepal. In: Working paper series, No. 22, Asia-Pacific research and training network on trade. http://www.unescap.org/tid/artnet

Matto A (2008) A handbook on international trade in services. Oxford University Press, New Delhi
Mattoo A (2001) Measuring service trade liberalisation and its impact on economic growth: an illustration. In: Policy research working paper 2655. World Bank, Washington, DC
Mattoo A (2006) Measuring services trade liberalization and its impact on economic growth. J Econ Integr 21(1):64–97
Mattoo A, Sauvé P (2003), Domestic regulations and trade in services: Key issues. In: Mattoo A, Sauvé P (eds) Domestic regulation & service trade liberalization. The World Bank, Washington DC
Ministry of Health (1991) National Health Policy, 1991. World Health Organization, Kathmandu
Ministry of Health (1999) Second long term health plan 1997–2017. Kathmandu
Ministry of Health (2003) Strategic plan for human resources for health 2003 to 2017. Government of Nepal, Kathmandu
Ministry of Health (2005) Annual report 2005. Department of Health Services, Kathamandu
Ministry of Health-Sri Lanka. National health strategic master plan 2016–2025, vol 4. Health Administration & HRH
Nepal Rastra Bank (2005) Nepal's WTO service sector commitments and its impact on balance of payment situation. Kathmandu, Nepal
Nessa A (2008) Applicability of telemedicine in Bangladesh: current status and future prospects. In: Conference proceedings, third international conference on convergence and hybrid information technology, pp 948–953
New Age (2006) New age. Daily Newspaper, Dhaka, Sunday, 8 Oct 2006
News Today (2005) Daily Newspaper, Thursday 11 Aug 2005
Nicolini D (2006) The work to make telemedicine work: a social and articulative view. Soc Sci Med 62:2754–2767
Nishtar S et al (2010) Protecting the poor against health impoverishment in Pakistan: proof of concept of the potential within innovative web and mobile phone technologies. World health report, background paper, vol 55. World Health Organization
OECD (2005) International development perspectives, vol 60. OECD Publications
Outreville JF (2007) Foreign direct investment in the health care sector and most-favored locations in developing countries. Eur J Health Econ 8:305–312
Pandey A (2017) Trends in catastrophic health expenditure in India: 1993 to 2014. Bull World Health Organ 96:18–28
Parasuraman A, Zeithamal VA, Berry LL (1988) SERVQUAL: a multiple item scale for measuring consumer perception of service quality. J Retail 64:12–40
Pavlovskaya O (2013) E-healthcare system coming to Kazakhstan (technical report). United States Central Command, Tampa, FL
Perkins D, Roemer M (1991) Reforming economic systems in developing countries. Harvard University Press, Boston
Prothom A (2009) Daily Newspaper, Monday, 6 July 2009
Rafiq A (2007) Telemedicine for access to quality care on medical practice and continuing medical education in a global arena. J Continuing Educ Health Prof 25:34–42
Rahman M (2000) Bangladesh-India bilateral trade: an investigation into trade in services. In: Paper prepared for SANEI. Centre for Policy Dialogue, Dhaka
Rahman M (2001) Bangladesh-India bilateral trade: an investigation into trade in services. Centre for Policy Dialogue, Dhaka
Rahman M (2002) Bangladesh-India bilateral trade: an investigation into trade in services. In: Srinivasan TN (ed) Trade, finance and investment in South Asia. SANEI and Social Science Press, New Delhi
Raihan A (2005) Liberalizing trade in services: negotiating strategy for Bangladesh. Centre for Policy Dialogue (CPD), Dhaka, Bangladesh
Raihan A, Mahmood M (2004) Trade negotiations on temporary movement of natural persons: a strategy paper for Bangladesh. In: Paper: 36, CPD occasional paper series. CPD, Dhaka

Rahman M, Bhattacharya D (2002) Trade potentials of South Asian economies under the new global trade regime: the role of some non-price factors—a case study of India, Bangladesh and Sri Lanka. Project Report for South Asia Network for Economic Research Institutes (SANEI), India

Ricardo B (2004) Comparative advantages of public and private providers in health care service in terms of cost, pricing, quality, and accessibility. Health Economics Unit, Ministry of Health and Family Welfare, Government of Bangladesh, Dhaka

SAARC Secretariat (2008) Report of the regional consultation meeting on the draft study on potential for trade in services under SAFTA agreement'. New Delhi, 6–7 February

Samaraweera D (2016) Meeting the current and future health-care needs of Sri Lanka's ageing population. WHO South-East Asia J Publ Health 5(2):96–101

SAWTEE (2008) Nepal's export potential in services: health, education and high-end retail services. Kathmandu

Smith R (2006) Measuring the globalization of health services: a possible index of openness of country health sector to trade. Health Econ Policy Law 1:323–342

The Daily Star (2008) Dhaka, Bangladesh

The Lancet (2002) vol 359, 20 Apr 2002, pp 1363–1364

UNCTAD (1997a) Report of the expert meeting on strengthening the capacity and expanding exports of developing countries in the services sector: health services. UNCTAD

UNCTAD (1997b) Health care exports under consumption abroad mode. Presentation on 16–18 June, Geneva

UNCTAD (1998) International trade in health services: difficulties and opportunities for developing countries, international trade in health services: a development perspective. UNCTAD-WHO Joint Publication, Geneva

UNCTAD (2005) International Investment agreements in services, UNCTAD/ITE/IIT/2005/2.UNCTAD, Geneva (2007). Trade in services and development implications, TD/B/COM.1/85, Geneva

UNCTAD (2008) Quantification of benefits from economic cooperation in South Asia. Macmillan India Limited, New Delhi

Unite for Universal Health Coverage: Sri Lanka (2019). Retrieved from https://www.facebook.com/sharer/sharer.php?u=http://www.ft.lk/healthcare/Unite-for-Universal-Health-Coverage-Sri-Lanka/45-668826

Wagstaff A (2014) Who benefits from government health spending and why? In: World Bank policy research working paper no. 7044. Washington, DC

Wagstaff A et al (2018) Progress on catastrophic health spending in 133 countries: a retrospective observational study. Lancet Glob Health 6:e169–e179

Waitzkin H (2005) Global trade, public health and health services: Stakeholders' constructions of key issues. Soc Sci Med 61:893–906

Whalley J (1985) Trade liberalization among major world trading areas. MIT Press, Cambridge Mass

Whalley J (1998) The division and size of gains from liberalization of service networks. In: National Bureau of economic research working paper, 6712

Whalley J (2000) What can the developing countries infer from the uruguay round models for future negotiations, policy issues in international trade and commodities. In: Study series no. 4. UNCTAD, New York and Geneva

WHO (undated) A methodological approach to assessing international trade in health services from a public health perspective. Division of Health System and Services Development Mediterranean Regional Office, World Health Organization, Cairo

WHO (2002) Trade in health service: global, regional and country perspective. WHO, Geneva

WHO (2006) The world health report. World Health Organization

Winters A (2002) Negotiating the liberalization of the temporary movement of natural persons. In: Discussion paper No. 87 (University of Sussex)

Winters A (2003) Liberalizing temporary movement of natural persons: an agenda for the development round. World Econ 26(8):1137–1161
World Bank (2003) Private sector assessment for health, nutrition and population (HNP) in Bangladesh report no: 27005-BD. World Bank, Washington, DC, pp 6–7
World Bank (2005) Comparative advantages of public and private health care providers in Bangladesh. Bangladesh development series—paper no. 4. www.worldbank.org.bd/bds
World Bank(2006) India-Bangladesh bilateral trade and potential free trade agreement. In: Bangladesh development series paper no: 13. www.worldbank.org.bd/bds
World Bank (2007) South asia growth and regional integration. The World Bank, Washington DC
World Health Organization, Organization for Economic Co-operation and Development and The World Bank (2018) Delivering quality health services: a global imperative for universal health coverage. Geneva
World Trade Organisation (WTO) (2001) Guide to the GATS: an overview of issues for further liberalisation of trade in services. Kluwer Law International, The Hague
WTO (2007) Challenges and opportunities in global services trade. International Trade Statistics
Zeithamal VA, Bitner MJ (2006) Marketing, 4th edn. McGraw-Hill/Irwin, Singapore

Websites Sources

ICDDR B (2007)
http://www.epb.gov.bd/bangladesh_country_profile.html#services
http://www.kuenselonline.com
http://info.worldbank.org/etools/wti2008/doc/indicators.htm
http://www.boi.gov.bd/boi_services.php
http://www.icddrb.org/pub/publication.jsp?classificationID=30&pubID=8848
Ministry of Health, Nepal. http://www.moh.gov.np
Shaptahik (2006) www.shaptahik2000.com
U. N. (undated) http://www.searo.who.int/en/Section313/Section1515_6124.htm
www.mohfwbdgov.org
www.epb.gov.bd
World Trade Organization. http://www.wto.org

The manufacturer's authorised representative in the EU is Springer Nature Customer Service Centre GmbH, Europaplatz 3, 69115 Heidelberg, Germany. If you have any concerns regarding our products, please contact ProductSafety@springernature.com

Printed and bound by CPI Group (UK) Ltd, Croydon, CR0 4YY
25/09/2026
02222901-0017